The HOLY SPIRIT
at WORK *in* YOU

The
HOLY
SPIRIT
at WORK *in* YOU

EUGENE H. LOWE, PH.D.

Orlando, Florida

The Holy Spirit at Work in You
by Eugene H. Lowe

Published by HigherLife Development Services, Inc.
2342 Westminster Terrace
Oviedo, Florida 32765
407-563-4806
www.ahigherlife.com

All scripture is taken from the New American Standard Bible®, copyright © The Lockman Foundation 1960, 1962, 1963, 1968, 1971, 1973, 1975, 1977, 1995. Used by permission. (www.Lockman.org)

ISBN: 978-0-9793227-9-2

Cover Design: Judith McKittrick Wright

First Edition
09 10 11 12 13 – 5 4 3 2 1
Printed in the United States of America

This book is dedicated to everyone who has, or will have, a desire for a deeper relationship with the Holy Spirit.

ACKNOWLEDGMENTS

Much of my free time for five-and-a-half years was consumed with researching, understanding, and organizing information; developing ideas; and then writing, editing, and re-editing the manuscript for this book. The inspiration and insights that I experienced were a great joy to me.

I thank my wife, Brenda, whom I love more than life itself, for her encouragement, help, and counsel, and for unselfishly allowing me the time for writing this book.

I am grateful for my friends the Reverend Claude Smithmier, E.J. "Woody" Clark, and Eric Forsgren, who provided me with insightful feedback on an early draft, and for Dr. Lee Edwards, who painstakingly edited a more mature draft.

I thank Dave Welday, who worked with me to turn the manuscript into a published book, and Deborah Poulalion, who edited the manuscript.

Finally, I thank my many other friends who encouraged me along the way.

CONTENTS

Section 6: Jesus—Anointed, Filled, and Empowered by the Holy Spirit

Section 7: Jesus' Earthly Ministry

Section 8: The Promise of the Holy Spirit

Section 9: Holy Spirit Baptism

Section 10: Indwelled and Filled with the Holy Spirit

Section 11: The Holy Spirit's Power

Section 12: The Will of God

Section 13: Led by the Holy Spirit

Section 14: Following the Holy Spirit

Section 15: The Gifts of the Holy Spirit

WHO IS THE HELPER?

T he place was Jerusalem, early spring, circa A.D. 30. For some time now, Jesus had been telling His disciples that He would soon be arrested, tried, condemned, and crucified. Then three days later, He would rise to life again. The disciples did not understand.

It had been an amazing week for the disciples, a week filled with excitement and anticipation. It began with Jesus' triumphal entry. As He rode into Jerusalem on a donkey, symbolic of a king coming in peace, throngs of people waved palm branches and shouted, "Hosanna to the Son of David! Blessed is He who comes in the name of the Lord!" (Matthew 21:9). Later in the week, Jesus single-handedly drove the livestock merchants and the moneychangers from the temple. This precipitated a confrontation with the chief priests, who challenged His authority to do such a thing.

When the day for sacrificing the Passover lamb arrived, Jesus and His disciples gathered in the Upper Room to share the Passover meal. His disciples did not realize that it would be their last such meal with Him.

Imagine that Jesus permitted you and me to stand near a doorway to the Upper Room. From our vantage point, we could see and hear everything that was happening inside. The meal had been a most holy occasion, as Jesus and the Twelve celebrated the anniversary of God's great miracle of deliverance. Also apparent was the remarkable intimacy of the fellowship within the room.

In the Upper Room

You and I watch as Jesus picks up a loaf of bread, holds it aloft, and blesses it. Then He breaks it and gives a piece to each of His disciples, telling them, "Eat this; it is My body which is given for you" (Luke 22:19).* Then He takes the cup, lifts it toward heaven, and gives thanks to God. He passes it among

---

* Lockman Foundation, *NASB*. (Author's paraphrase.)

His disciples, saying, "Drink this; it is My blood of the Covenant which is poured out for you" (22:20).*

Later we watch as Jesus takes a basin, a pitcher of water, and a towel and washes the disciples' feet. How unexpected; that was a servant's task! When Jesus finishes, He tells them that they should likewise wash one another's feet. They should serve one another in love and humility, just as He had done. What a remarkable moment!

Perhaps it is the holiness of this particular Passover, but whatever the reason, Jesus shares more deeply and profoundly than He ever has before. His words come from the very core of His innermost being. He says:

> But now I am going to Him who sent me…I tell you the truth, it is to your advantage that I go away; for if I do not go away, the Helper will not come to you; but if I go, I will send Him to you. [John 16:5a, 7]

We turn and stare at each other, stunned by what Jesus just said. We can't seem to help it; the words tumble out of one of us, "How can someone replace Jesus? How can anyone else's presence be better than His? And who is the Helper whom Jesus said He would send?"

The other of us replies, "Be quiet! Jesus is still speaking!" and we both turn back and listen intently:

> And He, when He comes, will convict the world concerning sin, and righteousness, and judgment: concerning sin, because they do not believe in Me; and concerning righteousness, because I go to the Father, and you no longer see Me; and concerning judgment, because the ruler of this world has been judged. [John 16:8–11]

Again we look at each other. We both wonder, "What does this mean?" Jesus continues:

> I have many more things to say to you, but you cannot bear them now. But when He, the Spirit of truth, comes, He will guide you into all the truth; for He will not speak on His own initiative, but whatever He hears, He will speak; and He will disclose to you what is to come. He will glorify Me; for He will take of Mine, and will disclose it to you. All things that the Father has are Mine; therefore I said that He takes of Mine and will disclose it to you. [16:12–15]

---

* *NASB.* (Author's paraphrase.)

I whisper, "It sounds like the Helper will be Jesus' representative with us here on earth and that Jesus will soon be returning to heaven!"

You reply, "Yes, that certainly sounds like what He is saying!"

WHO IS THE HELPER?

The information that Jesus shared about the Helper raises some very important questions. To begin with, who is the Helper whom Jesus said He would send? The short answer is that the Helper is the Holy Spirit. And who is the Holy Spirit? That question is not as easy to answer. A church council that met in A.D. 381 described Him this way in the Nicene Creed:

> And I believe in the Holy Ghost, the Lord, and Giver of Life, Who proceedeth from the Father and the Son; Who with the Father and the Son together is worshipped and glorified; Who spake by the Prophets....*

That answer is doctrinally correct, but it seems much too impersonal, and the Holy Spirit is the complete opposite of impersonal. He is warm and friendly and very approachable as He comes to us, ministers to us, and represents Jesus and the Father to us.

How shall we describe the Holy Spirit? He has such unity with and similarity to the Father and to Jesus that the Bible often refers to Him as the Spirit of God and as the Spirit of Jesus. During the Last Supper, Philip asked Jesus to show them the Father. Jesus replied that whoever has seen Him has seen the Father. The Father, Jesus, and the Holy Spirit are very much alike. Even so, they are distinct and they have distinct roles relative to us.

In the gospels Jesus was Emmanuel, meaning "God with us." At His ascension, Jesus returned to His place in heaven. Now the Holy Spirit is even more than God with us—He is God in us. Our bodies, both individually and corporately, are His temple.

What would most revolutionize our lives as followers of Jesus? It would be to know the Holy Spirit intimately, to continually experience His joy and peace, and to allow Him to work unimpeded through us in ministry to others. In this book I will show you ways that we can do that.

Many books about the Holy Spirit are written primarily from an individual's personal experience, but this book is not my autobiography. Instead it

---

* Wikipedia Foundation, Inc., *Nicene Creed*.

focuses on the Holy Spirit Himself and the work that He does. It presents an objective, Scriptural basis for understanding the Holy Spirit and how He can work in you today.

THE HOLY SPIRIT — AT WORK IN THE OLD TESTAMENT

Too often people have the impression that the Holy Spirit first began His work on the Day of Pentecost after Jesus had returned to heaven. However, starting with the moment of creation, the Holy Spirit was absolutely essential to everything that God accomplished throughout the Old Testament. In addition, all the truths about the Holy Spirit that we learn from the Old Testament apply to His activity today. In this book you will discover:

- The Holy Spirit's role in creation.
- How the Holy Spirit worked with Old Testament leaders and prophets.
- The Holy Spirit's prophecies about the coming of Jesus.
- Prophecies about the Holy Spirit's role subsequent to Jesus' ascension.

THE HOLY SPIRIT — IN PARTNERSHIP WITH JESUS

Another facet of the Holy Spirit is often overlooked as well—His cooperative relationship with Jesus Christ. Almost no books adequately address this topic. You will learn about the Holy Spirit's vital role in the incarnation and in the earthly ministry of Jesus. We will examine the ways that Jesus ministered under the leadership and in the power of the Holy Spirit, and see that God also intends for us to minister in those same ways. For example:

- Jesus was conceived by the Holy Spirit. We are born again, or made spiritually alive, by the Holy Spirit.
- The Father baptized Jesus with the Holy Spirit. Jesus baptizes us with the Holy Spirit.
- The Holy Spirit led Jesus. The Holy Spirit will also lead us.
- Jesus ministered in the power of the Holy Spirit. We too can minister in the power of the Holy Spirit.
- Jesus taught His disciples to pray. The Holy Spirit will help us pray.

- Jesus appoints us to spiritual ministries. The Holy Spirit then ministers His spiritual gifts through us.

God desires that we become more and more like Jesus. The Holy Spirit does the work of transforming us into the likeness of Jesus.

THE HOLY SPIRIT—AT WORK IN ALL BELIEVERS TODAY

The Book of Acts and the epistles are filled with practical information about how the Holy Spirit works in the life of every believer. However, to really understand the Holy Spirit, we must study the Scriptures comprehensively with an open mind and heart. This book does not focus on only one aspect of the Holy Spirit (such as who He is, how to talk to Him, or how to use His gifts and manifestations), but rather addresses all these areas. For example, you will learn:

- The difference between being indwelled by the Holy Spirit and being filled with the Holy Spirit.
- Three steps to take in order to follow the Holy Spirit.
- How to have fellowship with the Holy Spirit.
- What the gifts and fruit of the Spirit reveal to us about God's nature.
- Specific gifts of the Spirit that are needed for specific ministries.
- The importance of healings and miracles in authenticating the gospel message.

THE HOLY SPIRIT AT WORK IN YOU

Would you like to know the Holy Spirit, the One whom Jesus and the Father sent to be our Protector, our Mentor, our Confidant, and our Intimate Friend? Would you like to learn how to follow Him and experience His presence in your life? Would you like to be characterized by the love, joy, confidence, and inner peace that only God can provide? Would you like to minister more effectively to the needs of other people?

The Holy Spirit at Work in You will help you build a deeper and more intimate relationship with the Holy Spirit. You can read this book during your personal quiet time, or study it in a weekly small group meeting or Sunday school class. By applying God's Word, we can discover the joys of getting to know the Holy Spirit, experiencing His presence and His peace, fellowshipping with Him, being led and mentored by Him, and partnering with Him in ministry to other people.

THE HOLY SPIRIT FROM GENESIS THROUGH JUDGES

1–1

THE HOLY SPIRIT IN CREATION

The Bible opens by proclaiming, "In the beginning God created the heavens and the earth" (Genesis 1:1).

Is there anything more awe-inspiring than gazing upward at a sky bursting with stars on a clear, dark night? God existed before they did, and it was He who created them.

In the second verse of the Bible we observe the Holy Spirit, the subject of this book, already at work upon the earth.

> The earth was formless and void, and darkness was over the surface of the deep, and **the Spirit of God*** was moving over the surface of the waters. [Genesis 1:2]

Even though the earth was dark, empty, and formless, the Holy Spirit was not intimidated by its condition. He was not dismayed or discouraged, for He knew what the earth could become. The remainder of Genesis 1 describes God at work, transforming the earth through the power and with the perfection which only He possesses.

You may sometimes feel like your life is dark, empty, and formless, without sufficient meaning or purpose. Do not despair! The Holy Spirit is present with you! He is not intimidated by your condition. He is neither dismayed nor discouraged by it, for He knows what you can become. As you allow Him to work in your life, as you cooperate with Him, He will undertake and oversee the lifelong process of transforming you into the likeness of Jesus Christ.

1–2

BEZALEL

We usually associate God the Father with dramatic and spectacular events in the Bible such as the creation of the universe and all that is

---

* Throughout the book, I often put portions of Scripture verses in boldface for emphasis.

in it, the destruction of Sodom and Gomorrah, the ten plagues in Egypt, and the parting of the Red Sea. In contrast, the Holy Spirit works mostly in and through individuals. Moreover, the Holy Spirit often works through ordinary people like you and me.

Consider the construction of the tabernacle in the wilderness. The tabernacle was God's project: He planned it and commissioned it, intending that it would be a replica of the tabernacle that is in heaven. During God's time with Moses on Mount Sinai, God provided Moses with detailed plans for it. God even provided the material—items that Israel had brought with them when they left Egypt. It was God who selected the artisans and craftsmen who would fashion the tabernacle and its furnishings. He chose an obscure man named Bezalel to be its lead craftsman, and said of him:

> **I have filled him with the Spirit of God** in wisdom, in understanding, in knowledge, and in all kinds of craftsmanship, to make artistic designs for work in gold, in silver, and in bronze, and in the cutting of stones for settings, and in the carving of wood, that he may work in all kinds of craftsmanship. [Exodus 31:3-5]

It was the Holy Spirit who provided Bezalel with the wisdom, understanding, knowledge, and skills that he needed to fashion the artistic elements of the tabernacle. Bezalel needed to be in constant communication with the Holy Spirit throughout the entire construction process.

Likewise, God uses the Holy Spirit to impart the wisdom, understanding, knowledge, and skills that we need to accomplish the tasks to which God calls us. To be successful, we too must be in constant communication with the Holy Spirit.

God was very pleased with the tabernacle and visibly demonstrated His approval at its dedication.

> Then the cloud covered the tent of meeting, and the glory of the Lord filled the tabernacle. Moses was not able to enter the tent of meeting because the cloud had settled on it, and the glory of the Lord filled the tabernacle. [Exodus 40:34-5]

In the same way that the Holy Spirit worked through Bezalel and the other artisans and craftsmen to implement God's plan and fulfill God's purpose, He will work through you and me to accomplish the tasks and to fulfill the purposes that God has for us. And whenever the Holy Spirit accomplishes a work for God through ordinary people, the divine glory of God is revealed.

1–3

MOSES AND THE ELDERS

During the first part of the wilderness journey, Moses led Israel single-handedly. He had not yet developed delegation skills. The frustration and stress of his numerous responsibilities, compounded by the ceaseless complaining of the Israelites whom he was leading, finally overwhelmed him. Moses developed a bad case of job burnout. In fact, he became so disheartened that he asked God to kill him if things were not going to improve (Numbers 11:15). Moses needed the Holy Spirit to be his Helper. Moses also needed Holy Spirit-led people to whom he could delegate responsibilities. God had been patiently waiting for Moses to realize his need:

> The Lord therefore said to Moses, "Gather for Me seventy men from the elders of Israel, whom you know to be the elders of the people and their officers and bring them to the tent of meeting, and let them take their stand there with you. Then I will come down and speak with you there, and I will take of **the Spirit** who is upon you, and will put Him upon them; and they shall bear the burden of the people with you, so that you will not bear it alone." [Numbers 11:16–17]

Moses did as the Lord had instructed him.

> Then the Lord came down in the cloud and spoke to him; and He took of **the Spirit** who was upon him and placed Him upon the seventy elders. And when **the Spirit** rested upon them, they prophesied. [Numbers 11:25]

We can gather a number of valuable insights about the work of the Holy Spirit by studying this passage. Moses had been audibly called by God from the burning bush. God had personally directed each of Moses' moves during the time of the ten plagues in Egypt. It was through Moses that God led Israel out of bondage, climaxed by parting the Red Sea and then drowning Pharaoh's army. Later, God met twice with Moses on Mount Sinai, for forty days each time. The Bible says that God spoke to Moses face-to-face, as a man speaks to his friend.

The verses we just read clearly say that the Holy Spirit was upon Moses. He was continually with Moses, giving him guidance, wisdom, understanding, encouragement, and even solutions when he needed them. God is infinite, but we are finite. God never gets weary, but we do. He is without limitations, but we have many. So even though God met regularly with Moses face-to-face, and even though the Holy Spirit was continually with and upon him, Moses still reached the limits of his emotional and physical endurance. And when he called out to God for help, God was there. God is always there for us, as well.

When Moses selected the seventy elders and called them to an assembly, I do not believe he told them what God had planned. I believe he decided to let God surprise them. And what a surprise it was when God sovereignly put the Holy Spirit upon each of them! Can you imagine what that experience must have been like? What an assurance it must have been for them that God Himself was touching them through His Spirit and empowering them for their work ahead, as He often does today!

Watch what else happened:

> But two men had remained in the camp; the name of one was Eldad and the name of the other Medad. And **the Spirit rested upon them** (now they were among those who had been registered, but had not gone out to the tent), and they prophesied in the camp. [Numbers 11:26]

For whatever reason, those two elders had not assembled with the others, but that was of no consequence to God. They had been selected by Moses, so God put His Holy Spirit upon them. They experienced the same anointing that the other elders experienced. Isn't it wonderful to know that God can touch us with the Holy Spirit no matter where we are!

Let's look at one other occasion in Moses' life. When Moses was about 120 years old, having led Israel through forty years of wilderness travels and travails, God told Moses that his task was complete. It was time for him to come home. Moses did not protest. His single request was for God Himself to appoint his successor.

> So the Lord said to Moses, "Take Joshua the son of Nun, **a man in whom is the Spirit,** and lay your hand on him…" [Numbers 27:18]

Joshua was unquestionably the most qualified person to succeed Moses. He had been one of the original twelve spies who had gone into Canaan forty years earlier. He and Caleb were the only two spies who returned with a good report about the land. They encouraged Israel to trust God, go forward, and conquer the territory that God had promised to Abraham and his descendents. Joshua had faithfully served as Moses' right-hand man throughout the wilderness journey. But notice that to God, Joshua's most important leadership qualification was that the Holy Spirit dwelled in him.

God still feels the same way. We shall see again and again that being led by the Holy Spirit is absolutely essential to the success of the people whom God chooses to use—and that includes you and me!

1–4

SAMSON

From Moses through King David, the Holy Spirit came upon every God-appointed leader of Israel. The Holy Spirit anointed and empowered them to function in their calling. We can read about four excellent examples of this from the period when Israel was ruled by judges. The Holy Spirit came upon Othniel (Judges 3), Gideon (Judges 6), Jephthah (Judges 11), and Samson (Judges 13–16). Let's look at the ways the Holy Spirit worked through Samson.

God had great plans for Samson. Before Samson was conceived, God sent an angel to tell his mother that she would bear a son. Through the angel, God gave her specific instructions about rearing him, including that he was never to shave his head.

> Then the woman gave birth to a son and named him Samson; and the child grew up and the Lord blessed him. And **the Spirit of the Lord began to stir him**…[Judges 13:24–25a]

As Samson grew and matured, the Holy Spirit began to work through him. He frequently came upon Samson, enduing him with supernatural strength.

> However, his father and mother did not know that it was of the Lord, for He was seeking an occasion against the Philistines. Now at that time the Philistines were ruling over Israel. Then Samson went down to Timnah with his father and mother, and came as far as the vineyards of Timnah; and behold, a young lion came roaring toward him. **The Spirit of the Lord came upon him mightily,** so that he tore him as one tears a young goat though he had nothing in his hand…Then **the Spirit of**

> the Lord came upon him mightily, and he went down to Ashkelon and killed thirty of them [the Philistines] and took their spoil…When he came to Lehi, the Philistines shouted as they met him. And the Spirit of the Lord came upon him mightily so that the ropes that were on his arms were as flax that is burned with fire, and his bonds dropped from his hands. He found a fresh jawbone of a donkey, so he reached out and took it and killed a thousand men with it. [Judges 14:4–6a, 19a; 15:14–15]

It must have been exhilarating for Samson each time the Holy Spirit came upon him so mightily. Suddenly he received supernatural strength and nothing seemed impossible for him to overcome: no challenge, no danger, no foe.

We ordinarily assume that Samson was powerfully built, bulging with muscles, and extremely strong. We picture him as having a Mr. Universe sort of physique. The Bible doesn't describe his appearance, but it is intriguing to picture him as a weakling. If that were the case, it would make those incredible feats of strength when the Holy Spirit came upon him even more astonishing to those who witnessed them and almost unbelievable to those who merely heard about them.

Unfortunately, Samson had some character flaws that he never overcame. He was arrogant and so overly confident that instead of avoiding danger and temptation, he sought them out and flirted with them. Even more seriously, he never developed a personal relationship with the Holy Spirit, the One who was giving him supernatural strength. The fact that he took the Holy Spirit's presence and power for granted made Samson vulnerable.

His downfall came when he foolishly told Delilah, his Philistine lover, that his uncut hair was the secret of his strength. She sold this information to the Philistines, and they stealthily shaved his head as he slept on her lap. Samson's hair was not really his source of strength; the Holy Spirit was. But Samson's hair was the symbol of his commitment to God, and he betrayed that commitment. When the Philistines shaved his head, the Holy Spirit departed from him.

> She said, "The Philistines are upon you, Samson!" And he awoke from his sleep and said, "I will go out as at other times and shake myself free." But he did not know that the Lord had departed from him. Then the Philistines seized him and gouged out his eyes; and they brought him down to Gaza and bound him with bronze chains, and he was a grinder in the prison. [Judges 16:20–21]

What a tragic downfall! What lost potential! From that day forward, he was a blind prisoner, living in utter humiliation. But God is merciful and faithful, even when we bring self-inflicted tragedies upon ourselves as Samson did. God never forgot Samson and He never forgets us, even when we fail Him.

One day the Philistine leaders assembled for a celebration to honor their god. They sent for Samson so that they could amuse themselves by publicly humiliating him. The guards led him into the temple and stood him between two main structural pillars.

> Then Samson called to the Lord and said, "O Lord God, please remember me and please strengthen me just this time, O God, that I may at once be avenged of the Philistines for my two eyes." Samson grasped the two middle pillars on which the house rested, and braced himself against them, the one with his right hand and the other with his left. And Samson said, "Let me die with the Philistines!" And he bent with all his might so that the house fell on the lords and all the people who were in it. So the dead whom he killed in his death were more than those whom he killed in his life. [Judges 16:28–30]

God answered Samson's prayer. The Holy Spirit came upon him that final time, and with a mighty shout of victory, Samson died.

Samson's life illustrates three important lessons for us.

1) We must each develop a personal relationship with the Holy Spirit and honor His presence in our lives.
2) We must continually be on our guard against sin and against overconfidence.
3) We must never surrender our faith in God, for He is forever faithful. He can use us to the very end of our lives when we continue to make ourselves available to Him.

Section 2

THE HOLY SPIRIT AND SAMUEL, SAUL, AND DAVID

2–1

SAMUEL AND SAUL

Hannah had been childless for many years. She and her husband Elkanah made annual pilgrimages to Shiloh, where the Ark of the Covenant resided, to present sacrifices to the Lord and to worship Him. It was during one of those visits that Hannah burst into uncontrollable sobbing and begged God for a son. She vowed that she would, in turn, give him back to the Lord. God answered her prayer and in due time her first son was born. Samuel was only a few years old when Hannah and Elkanah returned to Shiloh and presented him to Eli the priest. After that, they only saw him during their annual visits to Shiloh.

Samuel was still a boy when he began ministering to the Lord under Eli's supervision. One night God spoke to Samuel audibly and said that He was bringing judgment upon Eli and his two sons. Eli's sons had been abusing their positions as priests by intimidating worshipers and confiscating portions of their offerings. Eli knew they were doing this, but he had done nothing to restrain them or discipline them. God's judgment came upon Eli and his sons, and all three died the same day.

Samuel grew and developed into a good and righteous man, so much so that God appointed him first as a prophet and later also as a judge of Israel. Time passed and Samuel in turn appointed his own sons as judges. That was a terrible mistake, for Samuel's sons became unscrupulous, just as Eli's sons had. They accepted bribes to pervert justice. It was Samuel's responsibility to discipline them and, if that did not succeed, to remove them from office. But Samuel, like Eli before him, could not bring himself to confront his sons, so he turned a blind eye to their misconduct.

The elders of Israel sought to remedy the problem, but instead of asking for God's counsel, they met and proposed their own solution. Their solution was to demand that Samuel appoint a king to rule over Israel. Samuel was devastated by their demand since, among other things, it would mean the end of his own judgeship. He prayed, and the Lord comforted him, saying, "They have not rejected you, but they have rejected Me from being king over them" (1 Samuel 8:7b).

Before the Lord agreed to the elders' request, He spoke to them through Samuel in his office as a prophet. God described the high price that Israel would pay if they chose to be ruled by an earthly king. The elders were adamant, however, and so the Lord selected Saul to be the first king of Israel.

The events that transpired next are described in 1 Samuel 9–10. Through a set of orchestrated circumstances, God arranged for Saul to seek out Samuel. Then God told Samuel that the man whom He had chosen to be Israel's first king would arrive the following day.

On the next day as Saul approached, God told Samuel that Saul was the man. The two met, and Samuel hinted to Saul that he was destined for greatness. Saul had no idea what this might mean. Samuel then invited Saul to be his guest at an upcoming feast and to spend the night in his home. Before the feast, he arranged for Saul to be seated with him in a place of honor at the head table.

The next morning as Saul prepared to return home, Samuel anointed him king of Israel, and then prophesied to him. The highlight of the prophecy was this:

> Afterward you will come to the hill of God...you will meet a group of prophets...and they will be prophesying. Then **the Spirit of the Lord will come upon you mightily,** and you shall prophesy with them and be changed into another man. [1 Samuel 10:5–6]

God had two purposes for giving Saul that prophecy and those signs. The first was to confirm that everything that would happen was God-ordained, and Saul would indeed become king of Israel. The second was to capture Saul's full attention. He wanted Saul to be alert, anticipating the day's climactic event—the Holy Spirit coming upon him.

> Then it happened when he turned his back to leave Samuel, God changed his heart; and all those signs came about on that day. When they came to the hill there, behold, a group of prophets met him; and **the Spirit of God came upon him mightily,** so that he prophesied among them. [1 Samuel 10:9–10]

God anointed Saul mightily with the Holy Spirit for two reasons: to provide him with access to the spiritual resources that he would need to function effectively as Israel's king; and to initiate the lifelong process of transforming Saul into all that he could become through God's guidance and grace. We have a comparable experience when we are born again. We are given access to spiritual resources, and it is the beginning of a lifelong transformation into all that we can become through God's guidance and grace. Like Saul, we do nothing to earn this gift; our part is simply to accept it.

Not long after that, the Ammonite army surrounded and besieged Jabesh-Gilead, one of the cities in Israel. The Ammonite king demanded that the city surrender, announcing that when it did, he would gouge out the right eye of every inhabitant of the city. The people of Jabesh-Gilead appealed for help to their fellow Israelites. God used that crisis to mobilize Israel and unite them behind Saul, for they had not yet accepted him as their king. Observe how the Holy Spirit worked:

> Then **the Spirit of God came upon Saul mightily** when he heard these words, and he became very angry. And he took a yoke of oxen and cut them in pieces, and sent them throughout the territory of Israel by the hand of messengers, saying, "Whoever does not come out after Saul and after Samuel, so shall it be done to his oxen." Then the dread of the Lord fell on the people, and they came out as one man. He numbered them in Bezek, and the sons of Israel were 300,000, and the men of Judah were 30,000. [1 Samuel 11:6–8]

Saul then led Israel to victory over the Ammonites, and Israel accepted him as their king.

You just read about two occasions when the Holy Spirit came upon Saul in a very powerful way. During the first, Saul prophesied and God changed his heart. During the second, Saul rallied Israel and led them to victory over the Ammonites. Despite those two dramatic incidents, Saul never made an effort to develop a personal relationship with the Holy Spirit. Saul never tried to get to know Him. Saul never learned how to listen to Him or be led by Him. As a result, very early in Saul's reign he sinned, and God sent Samuel to tell him that he was being rejected as king. Saul did not simply accept God's decision and resign. Instead, he clung to his position and continued to reign until his death in battle many years later.

Both Samson and Saul experienced the grace of God and the anointing of the Holy Spirit, but they took these gifts for granted. The tragedies that befell both men were the direct result of their willfulness and their failure to submit their lives to the leadership of the Holy Spirit. They stand in marked contrast to David, whom we shall study next.

2–2

DAVID

After rejecting Saul as king, God selected his successor. He sent Samuel to Bethlehem to anoint one of the sons of Jesse to be Israel's next king. However, God did not tell Samuel which son it was. Jesse had eight sons and he began presenting them to Samuel, beginning with the eldest. When Jesse finally got to David, the youngest, God showed Samuel that David was the one He had chosen. Notice what the Holy Spirit did:

> Then Samuel took the horn of oil and anointed him in the midst of his brothers; and **the Spirit of the Lord came mightily upon David from that day forward.** And Samuel arose and went to Ramah. Now **the Spirit of the Lord departed from Saul,** and an evil spirit from the Lord terrorized him. [1 Samuel 16:13–14]

Having the Holy Spirit come mightily upon David was an impressive confirmation to everyone gathered there that God had indeed chosen him as the next king of Israel. Notice what else verse 13 says, "the Spirit of the Lord came upon David mightily *from that day forward.*" The "Spirit of the Lord," or the Holy Spirit, would be David's greatest helper and ally throughout the remainder of his life. The Holy Spirit can be our greatest helper and ally, as well!

When the Holy Spirit departed from Saul, it was clear that God had rejected him as king. Such an event is very rare in Scripture. I could only find one other example: when the Holy Spirit departed from Samson (Judges 16:20). I admit that I do not understand what the Bible means when it says that an evil spirit from the Lord terrorized Saul, for I do not believe that the Lord assigns evil spirits to torment people. It is Satan who does that. However, the Lord can choose to remove His protection from a person, thereby allowing evil spirits to have unimpeded access to him. Perhaps that is what happened to Saul.

Some time later, Saul became obsessed with killing David. It was caused by a combination of jealousy and a desire to thwart God's plans. God's having chosen David to be Israel's next king meant that Saul's son Jonathan would not inherit the throne. When David learned that he was in mortal danger, he fled Jerusalem. An informant sent word to Saul that David was with Samuel in Ramah. That set the stage for what happened next.

In Genesis 6:3b, God declared, "My Spirit shall not strive with man forever." That verse reveals that one of the Holy Spirit's functions is to strive with people. Jesus said in John 16:8 that the Holy Spirit convicts people of sin and strives with them to bring them to repentance. With that in mind, notice how gently yet dramatically the Holy Spirit strives, first with Saul's messengers and later with Saul himself, to bring them to repentance.

> Then Saul sent messengers to take David, but when they saw the company of prophets prophesying, with Samuel standing and presiding over them, the Spirit of God came upon the messengers of Saul; and they also prophesied. When it was told Saul, he sent other messengers, and they also prophesied. So Saul sent messengers again the third time, and they also prophesied. [1 Samuel 19:20–21]

Saul's men were not expecting to be in the Lord's presence; they had been sent to arrest David so that Saul could have him executed. God protected David and He did it in a most unusual way: He allowed the messengers to experience His presence and His glory. As they approached Samuel and David, they became more and more aware of the Holy Spirit's presence. When they were near enough, they experienced His presence in such a powerful way that they began to prophesy. Afterward, they abandoned their mission and returned empty-handed.

Thwarted three times, Saul set out for Ramah to seize David himself. God then repeated the sequence of events with Saul:

> Then he himself went to Ramah, and came as far as the large well that is in Secu; and he asked and said, "Where are Samuel and David?" And someone said, "Behold, they are in Naioth in Ramah." He proceeded there to Naioth in Ramah; and **the Spirit of God came upon him** also, so that he went along prophesying continually until he came to Naioth in Ramah. He also stripped off his clothes, and he too prophesied before Samuel and lay down naked all that day and all that night. Therefore they say, "Is Saul also among the prophets?" [1 Samuel 19:22–24]

David's future suddenly seemed much brighter. It looked as if Saul might change his heart toward David as he experienced the glory of the Lord. The Holy Spirit had once again come upon Saul, the man from whom He had previously departed. What a contrast it must have been for Saul! The Holy Spirit was now upon him! The evil spirit that had tormented him had disappeared! Saul prophesied, lying prostrate on the ground before the Lord for a day and a night. During that time, the Holy Spirit was striving with him, urging him to repent. But sadly, it was an unrepentant Saul who arose and returned home the next day, never relenting in his quest to kill David. What a missed opportunity that was for Saul! David later became Israel's king, but Saul's refusal to repent of his murderous intentions doomed both him and his son Jonathan to death. And the Holy Spirit never again came upon Saul.

In marked contrast to Saul's attitude, initially ignoring and later actively resisting the Holy Spirit, David embraced Him and gratefully welcomed His presence. David was probably a teenager when Samuel anointed him to be king, and it would be many years before David ascended to the throne. But from the time the Holy Spirit first came so mightily upon David, He remained David's constant companion and source of strength. He was there in the good times and in the difficult times. He was there during the trials and during the victories. The Holy Spirit is available today to each of us to be our constant companion and our source of strength through the good times and the bad, through the trials and the victories.

David wrote many beautiful, profound, and anointed psalms that were based on his experiences. In some of them, he described his deep anguish as he experienced a betrayal or underwent a trial. Then he recorded what the experience had taught him about God's faithfulness. In others, he revealed aspects of his deep personal relationship with the Holy Spirit. Psalm 143, for example, contains David's prayer that the Holy Spirit would continue to teach him, lead him, and help him fulfill God's plan for his life:

> Teach me to do Your will,
> For You are my God;
> Let Your good Spirit lead me on level ground. [Psalm 143:10]

We would all do well to make this prayer ours.

If we allow ourselves to be vulnerable to circumstances that could tempt us to sin, then Satan will arrange for those circumstances to occur. That was what happened to David. One evening as he was looking over Jerusalem from his rooftop, he noticed an incredibly beautiful woman bathing. He inquired and found out that she was Bathsheba, the wife of Uriah, one of his military commanders. Uriah was away at war at the time.

David already had several wives. Nevertheless, he was so enthralled with Bathsheba's beauty that he sent for her, and what he had hoped for happened. Soon afterward, Bathsheba discovered that she was pregnant and sent word to David.

David tried to keep his sin from being discovered, but everything he tried failed. Finally, he ordered one of his military commanders to have Uriah killed and to make it look as if he had been a casualty of war. Temptation. Adultery. A cover-up. Murder. David sinned grievously! The Bible recorded it, and three thousand years later we are still shocked that a man of God could do such things. But he did, and God saw it all. Therefore, God sent the prophet Nathan to David, and it was a devastating confrontation. Psalm 51 records David's confession, his fervent prayer of repentance, and his heart-rending cry for mercy. It contains these two well-known verses:

> Create in me a clean heart, O God,
> And renew a steadfast spirit within me.
> Do not cast me away from Your presence,
> And do not take Your Holy Spirit from me. [Psalm 51:10–11]

Notice how David prayed. He implored God to cleanse his heart and his spirit. He begged not to be expelled from God's presence, for nothing could be worse punishment, then or now. He pleaded with God not to take the Holy Spirit from him. David knew that such punishments were real possibilities. He was acutely aware that God had punished Saul in those very ways after Saul sinned and God sent Samuel to confront him. Why were those things, above anything else, so important to David? It was because his intimate fellowship with God and his access to God in prayer and worship were so precious to David that he could not bear the thought of losing them. God answered David's prayer. He punished David but did not strip him of His fellowship.

In Psalm 139:7, David wrote, "Where can I go from Your Spirit? Or where can I flee from Your presence?" Yet in Psalm 51:11, David pleaded with God not to be expelled from His presence. At first glance, those verses seem to be contradictory, but closer examination reveals that they are not. You see, God can expel us from His presence if He so chooses. But if we try to flee from Him as Jonah did, we cannot escape. If we sin as Saul did, God may withdraw our awareness of the Holy Spirit's presence so that we can no longer fellowship with Him. But God loves us so much that He would never let us run away from the presence of the Holy Spirit.

David's psalms are so inspiring because he was able to clearly hear and faithfully write what the Holy Spirit spoke to him. They are, as the Apostle Paul describes in 2 Timothy 3:16, God-breathed. Many of David's psalms include profound prophecies about Jesus. Some examples are Psalms 16, 22,

24, and 110. Jesus often quoted from David's psalms as He explained spiritual truths. Examples include Psalm 6:8, 8:2, 22:1, 35:19, 41:9, 62:12, and 110:1. One man, David, who was completely yielded to the Holy Spirit, has for three thousand years helped people learn to trust God.

At the end of his life, David described his relationship with the Holy Spirit this way:

> Now these are the last words of David.
> David the son of Jesse declares,
> The man who was raised on high declares,
> The anointed of the God of Jacob,
> And the sweet psalmist of Israel,
> **"The Spirit of the Lord** spoke by me,
> And His word was on my tongue." [2 Samuel 23:1–2]

No other person in the Old Testament had a more intimate relationship with the Holy Spirit than did David. One result was that David later became recognized as one of history's greatest spiritual giants. And the Holy Spirit is still speaking through the psalms that David wrote and the events of David's life to instruct and enlighten and comfort people today.

David cannot possibly have realized the impact that he would have on future generations because of the ways the Holy Spirit worked through him during his lifetime. Nor can we!

THE HOLY SPIRIT AND
THE PROPHETS

3 – 1

THE OLD TESTAMENT PROPHETS

Biblical prophecies originated with God and were delivered by prophets speaking or writing under the inspiration of the Holy Spirit, as the Apostle Peter explained:

> But know this first of all, that no prophecy of Scripture is a matter of one's own interpretation, for no prophecy was ever made by an act of human will, but **men moved by the Holy Spirit spoke from God.** [2 Peter 1:20–21]

God can, and on occasion does, speak to people in an audible voice. He spoke to Moses from the burning bush and to Israel from Mount Sinai. He spoke at Jesus' baptism in the Jordan River and to Peter, James, and John on the Mount of Transfiguration. Jesus spoke to Saul on the road to Damascus. But instances such as those are rare, for God normally speaks to people through the Holy Spirit. The Holy Spirit moves upon someone and they prophesy, just as Peter described.

A prophet's ministry is to hear what God speaks to him through the Holy Spirit, and then deliver that message to its intended recipient. The recipient may be an individual, a group of people, a nation, or even all of mankind. The Bible contains many examples of prophecies to each type of recipient.

In this book we will often refer to Old Testament prophecies. It is important that we trust the accuracy and the authenticity of biblical prophecies, for they are foundational to our understanding of the ways the Holy Spirit has worked in the past and is working today. So that we may better appreciate the sovereignty of a prophet's calling, let's read how God called Isaiah.

> In the year of King Uzziah's death, I saw the Lord sitting on a throne, lofty and exalted, with the train of His robe filling the temple. Seraphim stood above Him, each having six wings; with two he covered his face, and with two he covered his feet, and with two he flew. And one called out to another and said,
>
> > "Holy, Holy, Holy is the Lord of hosts,
> > The whole earth is full of His Glory."

> And the foundations of the thresholds trembled at the voice of
>   him who called out, while the temple was filling with smoke.
>   Then I said,
> "Woe is me, for I am ruined!
> Because I am a man of unclean lips,
> And I live among a people of unclean lips;
> For my eyes have seen the King, the Lord of hosts."
>
> Then one of the seraphim flew to me, with a burning coal in his hand
> which he had taken from the altar with tongs. He touched my mouth
> with it and said, "Behold, this has touched your lips; and your iniquity is
> taken away, and your sin is forgiven."
> Then I heard the voice of the Lord, saying, "Whom shall I send, and
> who will go for Us?" Then I said, "Here am I. Send me!"
> He said, "Go, and tell this people…" [Isaiah 6:1–9a]

Notice that it was God who initiated Isaiah's vision; Isaiah was not seeking such an experience. And notice Isaiah's reaction when he found himself in God's presence: he was almost overcome by the recognition of his sinful nature. But God has a provision for cleansing us so that we can be accepted into His presence. For Isaiah, He dispatched an angel to apply a holy touch in the form of a burning coal from the altar. Isaiah was thereby declared to be cleansed of his iniquity and forgiven.

Next, God presented an opportunity to him by asking, "Who will go for Us?" Isaiah immediately and unreservedly volunteered to do whatever he could: "Here am I. Send me!" His assignment was to hear whatever God spoke and to deliver God's message to Israel.

God's Old Testament prophets took their callings and their responsibilities with the utmost seriousness. When they spoke prophetically, they spoke only what God had said—no more and no less. Because biblical prophecies are God's own messages, spoken or written by His prophets under the direct inspiration of the Holy Spirit, we can have complete confidence that they are true.

It is absolutely imperative that a prophet faithfully perform his ministry, for his obedience or disobedience can have eternal consequences. Notice how God explained Ezekiel's responsibilities and then described the potential consequences, both to the intended recipient of the message and to the prophet, if Ezekiel did not deliver God's warnings whether to the wicked or to the righteous.

Son of man, I have appointed you a watchman to the house of Israel; **whenever you hear a word from My mouth, warn them from me.** When I say to the wicked, "You will surely die," and you do not warn him or speak out to **warn the wicked** from his wicked way that he may live, that wicked man shall die in his iniquity, but his blood I will require at your hand. Yet if you have warned the wicked and he does not turn from his wickedness or from his wicked way, he shall die in his iniquity; but you have delivered yourself. Again, when a righteous man turns away from his righteousness and commits iniquity, and I place an obstacle before him, he will die; since you have not warned him, he shall die in his sin, and his righteous deeds which he has done shall not be remembered; but his blood I will require at your hand. However, if you have **warned the righteous man** that the righteous should not sin and he does not sin, he shall surely live because he took warning; and you have delivered yourself. [Ezekiel 3:17–21]

There will be times in our lives when we sense that God wants us to speak to someone on His behalf. It may be to tell him or her about Jesus. It may be to offer a word of comfort or encouragement. It may be to warn against some course of action. While God does not hold us to the same standard of obedience to which He held His Old Testament prophets, we must recognize that our acts of obedience or disobedience can have substantial, even eternal, consequences. Let us therefore be faithful to obey God whenever He gives us such an assignment.

In the following three chapters, I want to show you examples from three categories of Old Testament prophecies, examples that explicitly mention activities of the Holy Spirit. The categories are:

1) Prophecies calling people and nations to repent.
2) Prophecies foretelling the relationship between Jesus and the Holy Spirit.
3) Prophecies foretelling the coming of the Holy Spirit.

3–2

PROPHECIES CALLING PEOPLE AND NATIONS TO REPENT

God's objective never is to punish people or nations; it is to bring them to repentance and restoration. But if they will not repent after He has given them repeated warnings, He will indeed punish them. God spoke again and again through His Old Testament prophets to warn Israel, Judah, and the surrounding nations to repent and turn to Him or suffer severe consequences. The prophet Micah described the way in which the Holy Spirit spoke to Israel through him:

> On the other hand I am filled with power—
> With **the Spirit of the Lord**—
> And with justice and courage
> To make known to Jacob his rebellious act,
> Even to Israel his sin. [Micah 3:8]

Whenever Micah spoke or wrote under the anointing of the Holy Spirit, he sensed that anointing. He knew that God's warnings were just, and he was aware of the power in his words, as well as the courage he was exercising in delivering God's messages to an unreceptive nation.

Nehemiah summarized the way God repeatedly warned Israel through His prophets as they spoke or wrote under the inspiration of the Holy Spirit. Israel refused to heed God's warnings, and, as a result, God punished them by allowing other nations to conquer them.

> However, You bore with them for many years,
> And **admonished them by Your Spirit through Your prophets**,
> Yet they would not give ear.
> Therefore You gave them into the hand of the peoples of the lands.
>   [Nehemiah 9:30]

Zechariah addressed the same problem: Israel continued to refuse to heed God's warnings delivered by His prophets under the inspiration of the Holy Spirit. Therefore the Lord punished them severely.

But they refused to pay attention, and turned a stubborn shoulder and stopped their ears from hearing. They made their hearts like flint so that they could not hear the law and the words which **the Lord of hosts had sent by His Spirit through the former prophets;** therefore great wrath came from the Lord of hosts. [Zechariah 7:11–12]

On some occasions, God sent a prophet to confront an individual concerning his sin. We have already examined two such occasions: Samuel confronting Saul and Nathan confronting David. Although I will not be saying much more about warnings from God, it is important that we understand that God is not pleased when He speaks and we ignore what He says. Let us determine not to ignore Him or discount what He speaks to us, as Israel so often did and as Saul did. Instead, let us be like David, who acknowledged and accepted God's messages whenever He spoke, whether it was an encouraging message or a reproof.

3–3

PROPHECIES FORETELLING THE RELATIONSHIP BETWEEN JESUS AND THE HOLY SPIRIT

To Christians, one of the most important events in history was Jesus' coming to earth as Messiah and Savior. He did not arrive unannounced. God provided a prophetic foundation to enable us, together with those who came before us and those who will come afterward, to recognize Jesus' coming and His earthly ministry. An important key to understanding Jesus' roles as Messiah and as Savior is found in His relationship with the Holy Spirit. In the coming chapters we will look in more detail at a number of prophecies that portray their relationship. The following three prophecies are among the most important.

The Spirit of the Lord will rest on Him,
The spirit of wisdom and understanding,
The spirit of counsel and strength,
The spirit of knowledge and the fear of the Lord. [Isaiah 11:2]

This prophecy proclaims that the Holy Spirit will continuously rest upon Jesus during His earthly ministry. It also names seven characteristics of the Holy Spirit:

1) As the Spirit of the Lord, the Holy Spirit represents the Father and Jesus to us.
2) As the spirit of wisdom, He has all wisdom and He provides us with words of wisdom when we need them.
3) As the spirit of understanding, He helps us understand what the Bible says and ways to apply its teachings in our daily lives.
4) As the spirit of counsel, He is our personal Counselor.
5) As the spirit of strength, He makes God's power available to us when we need it.
6) As the spirit of knowledge, He has all knowledge and He provides us with words of knowledge when we need them.
7) As the spirit of the fear of the Lord, He teaches us to respect the Lord and to honor His Word, the Bible.

We will learn more about these characteristics of the Holy Spirit in later chapters.

The second key prophecy announced that the Father would anoint Jesus with the Holy Spirit for His earthly ministry.

> Behold, My Servant, whom I uphold;
> My chosen one in whom My soul delights.
> **I have put My Spirit upon Him;**
> He will bring forth justice to the nations. [Isaiah 42:1]

The Father Himself chose Jesus. Jesus would perform His earthly ministry as a servant, serving the Father's purposes. The prophecy also declared that the Father delights in Jesus, and it foretold that Jesus would one day bring justice to all the nations of the earth.

The third prophecy is the one that Jesus read in the synagogue in Nazareth to announce to the people of His hometown that His earthly ministry had begun. Jesus told them that this prophecy was about Him and His earthly ministry. Notice that the Holy Spirit was absolutely central to everything that Jesus would do.

The Spirit of the Lord God is upon me,
Because the Lord has anointed me
To bring good news to the afflicted;
He has sent me to bind up the brokenhearted,
To proclaim liberty to captives,
And freedom to prisoners;
To proclaim the favorable year of the Lord. [Isaiah 61:1–2a]

We will study these prophecies in more detail in later chapters.

3–4

PROPHECIES FORETELLING THE COMING OF THE HOLY SPIRIT

In the Old Testament, the Holy Spirit worked only through a select few of Israel's leaders and through God's prophets. But a time was coming when the Holy Spirit would work through everyone who was yielded to Him!

God said that He would *put His Holy Spirit within people*, simultaneously giving them a new heart that is attuned to Him and a new spirit that is alive to Him. This happens to us when we are born again.

> Moreover, I will give you a new heart and put a new spirit within you; and I will remove the heart of stone from your flesh and give you a heart of flesh. **I will put My Spirit within you** and cause you to walk in My statutes, and you will be careful to observe My ordinances. [Ezekiel 36:26–27]

There is more! God said that in addition to the new birth, He would *pour out His Spirit upon people* who thirst for more of Him.

> For I will pour out water on the thirsty land
> And streams on the dry ground;
> **I will pour out My Spirit on your offspring,**
> And My blessing on your descendants. [Isaiah 44:3]

One of the effects of this outpouring is to move us into a realm in which He can communicate with us supernaturally through dreams, visions, and prophetic messages.

> It will come about after this
> That **I will pour out My Spirit on all mankind;**
> And your sons and daughters will prophesy,
> Your old men will dream dreams,
> Your young men will see visions.
> Even on the male and female servants
> **I will pour out My Spirit in those days.** [Joel 2:28–29]

God pronounced that, unlike in Old Testament days, a time was coming when He would no longer impose limitations based upon gender, age, or status. He would pour out the Holy Spirit upon males and females and upon young people and old people, regardless of their status in life. That era began when the church was born on the Day of Pentecost, and it still continues today! In later chapters we will examine more closely what happened at Pentecost and afterward, and what that means for us who are living today.

Section 4

THE HOLY SPIRIT IN JESUS' INCARNATION

4 – 1

PROPHECIES ABOUT JESUS' BIRTH

Let us look next at the activities of the Holy Spirit that prepared the way for the birth of Jesus. God developed His plan for Jesus to come to earth long before Jesus' birth in Bethlehem. His plan's two main objectives were: to have Jesus demonstrate to us what God is like; and to have Jesus become our Savior by dying on a cross and atoning for our sins. The Holy Spirit, speaking especially through Moses, David, and the prophets, provided numerous clues about God's plan for the coming Messiah. From our perspective today, long after those events occurred, it seems easy to recognize prophecies that foretold them. But when they were first given under the inspiration of the Holy Spirit, even the prophets who delivered them did not fully comprehend what they meant, for Peter wrote:

> As to this salvation, the prophets who prophesied of the grace that would come to you made careful searches and inquiries, seeking to know what person or time **the Spirit of Christ*** within them was indicating as He predicted the sufferings of Christ and the glories to follow. It was revealed to them that they were not serving themselves, but you, in these things which now have been announced to you through those who preached the gospel to you by **the Holy Spirit** sent from heaven—things into which angels long to look. [1 Peter 1:10–12]

Jesus fulfilled many biblical prophecies as part of His earthly ministry. He fulfilled others during His betrayal, trial, crucifixion, and resurrection. Yet after His resurrection, there were still many prophecies to be fulfilled. They included: the coming of the Holy Spirit, the birth of the church, Jesus' Second Coming, and the eternal kingdom of God. We will address some of those later, but for right now let's return our attention to the activities of the Holy Spirit in preparing for the birth of Jesus.

---

* When we are reading familiar Bible verses, most of us have the tendency to see in them only what we have always seen and to interpret them as we have always interpreted them. If we do that with the verses that we will study in the upcoming chapters, we will miss many wonderful insights into who the Holy Spirit is and the way in which He works. To underscore what the Bible says about Him, I often put His name in boldface in the Scripture verses.

It was around the year 1000 B.C. when the Lord spoke through the prophet Nathan and promised King David that the Messiah would be one of his descendants.

> Your house and your kingdom shall endure before Me forever; your throne shall be established forever. [2 Samuel 7:16]

Roughly three hundred years later, the Lord spoke through Isaiah concerning the Messiah's virgin birth.

> Therefore the Lord Himself will give you a sign: Behold, a virgin will be with child and bear a son, and she will call His name Immanuel. [Isaiah 7:14]

That title *Immanuel* means "God with us."

The Holy Spirit confirmed through Isaiah that the Messiah would be a descendant of David. Isaiah's prophecy added information of paramount importance: the Holy Spirit would be upon Him.

> Then a shoot will spring from the stem of Jesse,
> And a branch from his roots will bear fruit.
> **The Spirit of the Lord** will rest on Him,
> The spirit of wisdom and understanding,
> The spirit of counsel and strength,
> The spirit of knowledge and the fear of the Lord. [Isaiah 11:1–2]

Around that same time, the Lord spoke through the prophet Micah and revealed that the Messiah would be born in David's hometown of Bethlehem.

> But as for you, Bethlehem Ephrathah,
> Too little to be among the clans of Judah,
> From you One will go forth for Me to be ruler in Israel.
> His goings forth are from long ago,
> From the days of eternity. [Micah 5:2]

More than one hundred years after that, the Lord sent word to the prophet Daniel through the angel Gabriel and revealed the time frame when the Messiah would be born.

> So you are to know and discern that from the issuing of a decree to restore and rebuild Jerusalem until Messiah the Prince there will be seven weeks and sixty-two weeks…[Daniel 9:25a]

Those 69 weeks are generally interpreted to be 69 periods of seven years, a total of 483 years. In the year 538 B.C., King Cyrus of Persia issued a decree to rebuild the temple in Jerusalem and two years later, Zarubbabel led the first group of Jewish exiles there from Babylon. In 445 B.C., King Artaxerxes of Persia issued a decree to rebuild Jerusalem's walls and gate, and Nehemiah led a second group of Jewish exiles from Babylon to Jerusalem. Doing some simple math (i.e., 483 years after the period of 538 B.C. to 445 B.C.), we can bracket the Messiah's coming. It would be between the years 55 B.C. and A.D. 38.

Summarizing those prophecies, the Messiah would be born in Judea, in the city of Bethlehem, to parents who were descendants of King David, sometime between 55 B.C. and A.D. 38. Do you find it as fascinating as I do to see how accurately biblical prophecy described the circumstances of Jesus' birth hundreds of years ahead of time?

4–2

ZACHARIAS AND ELIZABETH

About fifteen months before Jesus was born, God's eternal plan of salvation swung into action. The opening events are described in Luke 1. The angel Gabriel, who had told Daniel when the Messiah would be born, visited a priest named Zacharias while he was ministering in the temple. Gabriel announced to Zacharias that:

- His wife Elizabeth would soon bear the son for whom they had been praying.
- They were to name him John.
- Zacharias would experience great joy.
- Many would rejoice at John's birth.

Gabriel continued, saying that:

- John would be great in the Lord's eyes.
- He would drink no wine or liquor.
- He would be filled with **the Holy Spirit** while he was still in his mother's womb.

Then Gabriel described John's ministry:

- John would turn many in Israel back to the Lord.
- He would be a forerunner of the Messiah.
- He would minister in the spirit and power of Elijah.
- His overall purpose was to prepare Israel for the coming of the Messiah.

Zacharias was struck dumb because he did not believe what Gabriel told him. When his period of priestly service was complete, he returned home. Elizabeth became pregnant soon afterward.

When the angel Gabriel visited Mary, he told her that her relative Elizabeth, who had previously been barren, was now in her sixth month of pregnancy. Although the Bible doesn't mention this fact, it is likely that Gabriel also told Mary about John the Baptist's role in preparing Israel for the coming of the Messiah. If so, that would help explain why Mary left so suddenly to go visit Elizabeth.

> Now at this time Mary arose and went in a hurry to the hill country, to a city of Judah, and entered the house of Zacharias and greeted Elizabeth. When Elizabeth heard Mary's greeting, the baby leaped in her womb; and Elizabeth was filled with **the Holy Spirit**. [Luke 1:39–41]

The moment Mary arrived, Elizabeth and John were filled with the Holy Spirit, fulfilling Gabriel's prophecy to Zacharias that John would be filled with the Holy Spirit while he was still in his mother's womb. There are three important points for us to notice about this event. First, it was God who filled John with the Holy Spirit. Gabriel had told Zacharias that John would minister in the spirit and power of Elijah. John would be able to do that because he would be empowered by the same Holy Spirit who had empowered Elijah. Second, John leaped for joy in Elizabeth's womb. Even as an unborn child, he experienced the joy of the Holy Spirit. Third, Elizabeth's immediate response to being filled with the Holy Spirit was to shower blessings upon Mary and Jesus.

> And she cried out with a loud voice, and said, "Blessed are you among women, and blessed is the fruit of your womb!" [Luke 1:42]

The Holy Spirit must have revealed to Elizabeth that Mary would be the mother of the Messiah, for Elizabeth asked: "And how has it happened to me, that the mother of my Lord would come to me?" (Luke 1:43). Elizabeth then continued to bestow blessings upon Mary: "And blessed is she who believed that there would be a fulfillment of what had been spoken to her by the Lord" (Luke 1:45).

Mary's response to Elizabeth's blessings and to the presence of the Holy Spirit was to give heart-felt praise to God and to declare His mighty works. It was recorded in Luke 1:46–55. Often referred to as the "Magnificat,"* Mary offered to God some of the most beautiful, Holy-Spirit-inspired praise in the entire New Testament.

Mary stayed with Zacharias and Elizabeth for about three months and then returned home. Shortly afterward the child was born, and at his circumcision he was given the name John. Zacharias' ability to speak was immediately restored, and the first words out of his mouth were praises to God. God's response to Zacharias' praises was to fill him with the Holy Spirit. Zacharias, Elizabeth, and John became the first Spirit-filled family in the New Testament. They were the recipients of an experience that God now makes available to every willing believer.

Zacharias, who was a priest but not a prophet, then spoke prophetically about Jesus. It is one the most powerful and inspiring prophecies about Jesus in all of Scripture. The prophecy also described how John the Baptist would be used to prepare Israel for Jesus' coming:

> And his father Zacharias was filled with **the Holy Spirit,** and prophesied, saying:
>
> > "Blessed be the Lord God of Israel,
> > For He has visited us and accomplished redemption for His people,
> > And has raised up a horn of salvation for us
> > In the house of David His servant—
> > As He spoke by the mouth of His holy prophets from of old—

---

* Merriam Webster, *Magnificat.*

Salvation from our enemies,
And from the hand of all who hate us;
To show mercy toward our fathers,
And to remember His holy covenant,
The oath which He swore to Abraham our father,
To grant us that we, being rescued from the hand of our enemies,
Might serve Him without fear,
In holiness and righteousness before Him all our days.
And you, child, will be called the prophet of the Most High;
For you will go on before the Lord to prepare His ways;
To give to His people the knowledge of salvation
By the forgiveness of their sins,
Because of the tender mercy of our God,
With which the Sunrise from on high will visit us,
To shine upon those who sit in darkness and the shadow of
  death,
To guide our feet into the way of peace." [Luke 1:67–79]

It would be intriguing to know more about the ways Zacharias and Elizabeth nurtured and guided and taught their son during his formative years, helping prepare him for his God-ordained ministry. The Bible does not share those details with us. Luke's gospel concludes the passage about John the Baptist by saying, "And the child continued to grow and to become strong in spirit, and he lived in the deserts until the day of his public appearance to Israel" (Luke 1:80).

4–3

MARY

When Elizabeth was in her sixth month of pregnancy, the angel Gabriel visited Mary. He announced to her that:

- She was favored by God.
- The Lord was with her.
- She would be the mother of the Messiah.
- She was to name Him Jesus.
- She would conceive through **the Holy Spirit** and the power of God.

Gabriel then described what Jesus would be like:

- He would be great.
- He would be called the Son of God.
- God would give Him the everlasting throne that He had promised to a descendant of David.
- He would reign over Israel forever.
- His kingdom would never end.

Very soon after Gabriel appeared to Mary, she went to visit Elizabeth and stayed with her for about three months. By the time Mary returned home, she knew that she was pregnant. When she told Joseph everything that had happened, he did not believe her. In fact, he was devastated by her seeming infidelity, the only other plausible explanation for her pregnancy. Matthew's gospel describes it this way:

> Now the birth of Jesus Christ was as follows: when His mother Mary had been betrothed to Joseph, before they came together she was found to be with child by **the Holy Spirit.** And Joseph her husband, being a righteous man and not wanting to disgrace her, planned to send her away secretly. But when he had considered this, behold, an angel of the Lord appeared to him in a dream, saying, "Joseph, son of David, do not be afraid to take Mary as your wife; for the Child who has been conceived in her is of **the Holy Spirit.** She will bear a Son; and you shall call His name Jesus, for He will save His people from their sins." [Matthew 1:18–21]

Matthew's gospel then refers to the prophecy in Isaiah 7:14,

> Now all this took place to fulfill what was spoken by the Lord through the prophet: "Behold, the Virgin Mary shall be with Child and shall bear a Son, and they shall call his name Immanuel," which translated means, "God with us." [1:22–23]

Mary (whose lineage is recorded in Luke 3:23–38) and Joseph (whose lineage is recorded in Matthew 1:2–16) were both descendants of David. Because Mary was Jesus' only earthly biological parent, it was necessary that she be a descendant of David to fulfill biblical prophecy. It was also important that Joseph be a descendant of David because God used that fact to cause the young couple to travel to David's hometown and fulfill Micah's prophecy that the Messiah would be born in Bethlehem:

> Now in those days a decree went out from Caesar Augustus, that a census be taken of all the inhabited earth. This was the first census taken while Quirinius was governor of Syria. And everyone was on his way to register for the census, each to his own city. Joseph also went up from Galilee, from the city of Nazareth, to Judea, to the city of David which is Bethlehem, because he was of the house and family of David, in order to register, along with Mary, who was engaged to him, and was with child. While they were there, the days were completed for her to give birth. And she gave birth to her firstborn son; and she wrapped Him in cloths, and laid Him in a manger, because there was no room for them in the inn. [Luke 2:1–7]

All of heaven witnessed Jesus' birth and rejoiced greatly that the long-awaited event had taken place. On earth, it was a lonely and private occasion for Mary and Joseph. The Bible gives us no hint that there were any family members or friends there to share the experience or to help and encourage the new parents. Nevertheless, God let them know that He knew. He encouraged them through a most unlikely source: a group of shepherds. Read the account in Luke 2:8–20, noticing especially verse 19, which says that Mary treasured the things the shepherds told her and pondered them in her heart. Mary is a marvelous example for us of someone with a serene faith and a complete trust in God.

4–4

SIMEON

On the eighth day after His birth, in accordance with the Law (see Leviticus 12:1–3), Mary and Joseph took their son to be circumcised. In obedience to what Gabriel had told Mary, as well as what an angel had told Joseph in a dream, they named Him Jesus. When her time of purification was complete (see 12:4), Mary went with Joseph to present Jesus to the Lord in the temple in Jerusalem according to the Law (see Exodus 13:2, 12 and Leviticus 12:6–8). Meanwhile, the Holy Spirit had been working quietly in Jerusalem, preparing for that day:

> And there was a man in Jerusalem whose name was Simeon; and this man was righteous and devout, looking for the consolation of Israel;

and **the Holy Spirit** was upon him. And it had been revealed to him by **the Holy Spirit** that he would not see death before he had seen the Lord's Christ. And he came in **the Spirit** into the temple; and when the parents brought in the child Jesus, to carry out for Him the custom of the Law, then he took Him into his arms, and blessed God, and said…[Luke 2:25–28]

Before we read what Simeon said, look with me at the way the Bible describes Simeon. It says that he was a righteous and devout man. He earnestly watched for the coming of the Messiah. The Holy Spirit was upon him and had revealed to him that not only would the Messiah come during his lifetime, but that also he would get to see the Messiah! Can you imagine what a thrilling moment it must have been when the Holy Spirit revealed that to him? Afterwards he must have been constantly energized, wondering each day if it would be *the* day.

Finally the day arrived, and the Holy Spirit led him to go to the temple. There He was—a baby in His mother's arms. With the anointing of the Holy Spirit upon him, Simeon took Jesus into his arms, gave thanks and praises to God, and spoke prophetically:

> "Now Lord, You are releasing Your bond-servant to depart in
>   peace,
>   According to Your word;
>   For my eyes have seen Your salvation,
>   Which You have prepared in the presence of all peoples,
>   A light of revelation to the Gentiles,
>   And the glory of Your people Israel."

> And His father and mother were amazed at the things which were being said about Him. And Simeon blessed them and said to Mary His mother, "Behold, this Child is appointed for the fall and rise of many in Israel, and for a sign to be opposed—and a sword will pierce even your own soul—to the end that thoughts from many hearts may be revealed." [Luke 2:29–35]

Simeon's Holy Spirit-anointed prophecy became an anchor point for Mary's faith. It was another specific message from God that she could hold in her heart. If we will become like Simeon—righteous, devout, and attentive to the Holy Spirit—the Lord will also use us in significant ways to bless others.

THE HOLY SPIRIT IN JOHN THE BAPTIST'S LIFE AND MINISTRY

5–1

JOHN THE BAPTIST

When Jesus began His public ministry, there was a bold, dynamic prophet and preacher in Judah who was drawing large crowds. John the Baptist had a fire-and-brimstone style of preaching, and the entire Jewish nation felt the impact of his ministry.

The angel Gabriel had announced his birth to his father Zacharias:

> And an angel of the Lord appeared to him, standing to the right of the altar of incense. Zacharias was troubled when he saw the angel, and fear gripped him. But the angel said to him, "Do not be afraid, Zacharias, for your petition has been heard, and your wife Elizabeth will bear you a son, and you will give him the name John. You will have joy and gladness, and many will rejoice at his birth. For he will be great in the sight of the Lord; and he will drink no wine or liquor; and he will **be filled with the Holy Spirit, while yet in his mother's womb.** [Luke 1:11–15]

Gabriel's announcement about John and the Holy Spirit was absolutely stunning. The Old Testament records many instances of the Holy Spirit *coming upon* a person. We studied some of them earlier. But there were only two people in the Old Testament that God said He *filled* with His Spirit: Bezalel (Exodus 31:3 and 35:31), the lead craftsmen for the construction of the Tabernacle, and Joshua (Numbers 27:18; Deuteronomy 34:9), Moses' successor. For Gabriel to announce that John would "be filled with the Holy Spirit, while yet in his mother's womb" was entirely without precedent. God was now doing a new thing, something He had prophesied through Ezekiel:

> I will put **My Spirit within you** and cause you to walk in My statutes, and you will be careful to observe my ordinances. [Ezekiel 36:27]

One aspect of Gabriel's announcement was fulfilled when Mary arrived at Elizabeth and Zacharias' home.

> When Elizabeth heard Mary's greeting, the baby **leaped in her womb;** and Elizabeth was filled with **the Holy Spirit.** [Luke 1:41]

John was filled with the Holy Spirit even before he was born!

Because his father Zacharias was a priest, John was born into the priest-hood. But instead of ministering in priestly garments, he wore a simple one-piece tunic woven of camel hair, secured by a leather belt. Instead of ministering in the temple in Jerusalem with the other priests, he ministered alone in the Judean wilderness. Instead of eating from the priest's portions of the offerings of lambs, bread, and wine, he ate locusts and wild honey.

Jesus said that of everyone born of a woman, no one was greater than John the Baptist. He was the only prophet, besides Jesus, whose ministry was foretold in the Old Testament. Isaiah prophesied about him and his role in preparing Israel for the coming of the Messiah:

> A voice is calling,
> "Clear the way for the Lord in the wilderness;
> Make smooth in the desert a highway for our God.
> Let every valley be lifted up,
> And every mountain and hill be made low;
> And let the rough ground become a plain,
> And the rugged terrain a broad valley;
> Then the glory of the Lord will be revealed,
> And all flesh will see it together;
> For the mouth of the Lord has spoken." [Isaiah 40:3–5]

John the Baptist was fully aware of his calling. The gospel of John describes an incident when a group of priests and Levites came from Jerusalem and asked him who he was. He answered them by quoting from this prophecy: "He said, 'I am a voice of one crying in the wilderness, "Make straight the way of the Lord,"' as Isaiah the prophet said" (John 1:23).

There are also prophecies about John the Baptist in the book of Malachi. The first links him to Jesus and declares:

> "Behold, I am going to send My messenger, and he will clear the way before Me. And the Lord, whom you seek, will suddenly come to His temple; and the messenger of the covenant, in whom you delight, behold, He is coming," says the Lord of hosts. [Malachi 3:1]

At John's circumcision, his father's prophecy applied that scripture to him: "And you, child, will be called the prophet of the Most High; For you will go on before the Lord to prepare His ways..." (Luke 1:76).

Jesus confirmed that this scripture was about John the Baptist when He said: "This is the one about whom it is written, 'Behold, I send My messenger ahead of You, who will prepare Your way before You'" (Matthew 11:10).

The second prophecy about John the Baptist in the book of Malachi consists of the last two verses in the Old Testament. That prophecy says that Elijah the prophet would come again. Elijah was one of the two people in the Old Testament (Enoch being the other) who did not die. He was taken to heaven in a whirlwind, as described in 2 Kings 2. Malachi prophesied:

> Behold, I am going to send you Elijah the prophet before the coming of the great and terrible day of the Lord. He will restore the hearts of the fathers to their children and the hearts of the children to their fathers, so that I will not come and smite the land with a curse. [Malachi 4:5–6]

When Gabriel announced to Zacharias that Elizabeth would conceive and bear a son, Gabriel applied Malachi's prophecy to John:

> And he will turn many of the sons of Israel back to the Lord their God. It is he who will go as a forerunner before Him in the spirit and power of Elijah, to turn the hearts of the fathers back to the children, and the disobedient to the attitude of the righteous, so as to make ready a people prepared for the Lord. [Luke 1:16–17]

Jesus confirmed that this prophecy was about John the Baptist when He said, "For all the prophets and the Law prophesied until John. And if you are willing to accept it, John himself is Elijah who was to come" (Matthew 11:13–14).

After John the Baptist was beheaded and not long before Jesus' crucifixion, Jesus took Peter, James, and John to the top of a mountain. There Jesus was transfigured and the disciples saw Him talking with Moses and Elijah. As the disciples descended from the mountain, having just seen Elijah, they asked Jesus to explain Malachi 4:5–6 to them:

> And His disciples asked Him, "Why then do the scribes say that Elijah must come first?" And He answered and said, "Elijah is coming and will restore all things; but I say to you that Elijah already came, and they did not recognize him, but did to him whatever they wished. So also the Son of Man is going to suffer at their hands." Then the disciples understood that He had spoken to them about John the Baptist. [Matthew 17:10–13]

Let's summarize what we have learned so far about the Holy Spirit's activities in John the Baptist's life and ministry. They began with the Holy Spirit speaking prophetically about John through Isaiah and through Malachi. Shortly before John was conceived, Gabriel announced that John would be filled with the Holy Spirit while he was still in his mother's womb. The Holy Spirit fulfilled that prophecy when Mary visited Elizabeth. At John's circumcision, the Holy Spirit came upon Zacharias, who then prophesied that John was God's chosen messenger to usher in Jesus' earthly ministry. As an adult, John the Baptist ministered in the spirit and power of Elijah. That is, he preached under the same Holy Spirit anointing as had the great prophet Elijah. When John baptized Jesus, he saw the Holy Spirit descend in the form of a dove and rest upon Jesus.

5–2

WHAT JOHN THE BAPTIST SAID ABOUT JESUS

John the Baptist—the prophet whose birth was announced by Gabriel, who was filled with the Holy Spirit while he was still in his mother's womb, whose ministry was prophesied by both Isaiah and Malachi, who was sent by God to prepare the world for the coming of the Messiah, the one to whom Jesus went to be baptized, who according to Jesus was the last Old Testament prophet—what did he have to say about Jesus?

John the Baptist's messages about Jesus are highly authoritative and of great significance to us. He made three extremely important pronouncements:

1) Jesus is the Lamb of God.
2) Jesus is much greater than John the Baptist.
3) Jesus will baptize people with the Holy Spirit.

1) JESUS IS THE LAMB OF GOD

John the Baptist's first pronouncement about Jesus was that He is the Lamb of God: "The next day he saw Jesus coming to him, and said, 'Behold, the Lamb of God who takes away the sin of the world!'" (John 1:29).

Again the next day John was standing with two of his disciples, and he looked at Jesus as He walked, and said, "Behold, the Lamb of God!" [John 1:35–36]

John the Baptist could unequivocally declare Jesus was the Lamb of God because God had revealed to him that Isaiah was speaking about Jesus when he prophesied:

He was oppressed and He was afflicted,
Yet He did not open His mouth;
Like a lamb that is led to slaughter,
And like a sheep that is silent before its shearers,
So He did not open His mouth. [Isaiah 53:7]

As the Lamb of God, Jesus was the perfect sacrifice to atone for sin—not just yours and mine, but everyone's! Jesus fulfilled Isaiah's prophecy during His trial and crucifixion. Philip the evangelist began with that prophecy when he preached about Jesus to the Ethiopian official in Acts 8:26–38.

The Apostle Peter referred to Christ as the spotless Lamb of God in his first letter:

Knowing that you were not redeemed with perishable things like silver or gold from your futile way of life inherited from your forefathers, but with precious blood, as of a lamb unblemished and spotless, the blood of Christ. [1 Peter 1:18–19]

In Revelation, the Apostle John described his vision of the four living creatures and the twenty-four elders in heaven as they fell down and worshiped Jesus the Lamb:

And I saw between the throne (with the four living creatures) and the elders a Lamb standing, as if slain...When He had taken the book, the four living creatures and the twenty-four elders fell down before the Lamb...And they sang a new song, saying,
    "Worthy are You to take the book, and to break its seals; for You were slain, and purchased for God with Your blood men from every tribe and tongue and people and nation. You have made them to be a kingdom and priests to our God; and they will reign upon the earth." [Revelation 5:6a, 8a, 9–10]

John the Baptist said it: Jesus is the Lamb of God. He is our Redeemer, and what a wonderful Redeemer He is!

2) JESUS IS MUCH GREATER THAN JOHN THE BAPTIST

John the Baptist's second pronouncement was so important that it was recorded in all four gospels. In three of the gospels, John declared that One was coming who was mightier than he (Matthew 3:11, Mark 1:7, Luke 3:16). To put this into perspective, John the Baptist said that he was not even worthy to serve Jesus by helping Jesus remove His sandals, which was a servant's task. In John 1:30, John said of Jesus, "This is He on behalf of whom I said, 'After me comes a Man who has a higher rank than I, for He existed before me.'"

Note those comparisons. Jesus had said that no one in all of mankind was greater than John the Baptist. Then John the Baptist said that Jesus was so much mightier than he was that he was not even worthy to help Him remove His sandals. What a mighty Jesus we serve!

3) JESUS WILL BAPTIZE PEOPLE WITH THE HOLY SPIRIT

John the Baptist's third pronouncement was also so important that it was recorded in all four gospels. In Mark, John the Baptist prophesied about the One coming after him, "I baptized you with water; but He will baptize you with **the Holy Spirit**" (1:8).

John's baptizing with water was symbolic of the cleansing work that the Holy Spirit does in our lives. Baptism with water also pointed to what Jesus would do: baptize us with the Holy Spirit. In Matthew 3:11 and in Luke 3:16, John the Baptist prophesied that the One coming after him would baptize with the Holy Spirit and fire. Fire is symbolic of the Holy Spirit's refining and purifying work in our lives.

In John's gospel, John the Baptist explained that he had not yet recognized Jesus as the Messiah when Jesus came to him to be baptized:

> "I did not recognize Him, but so that He might be manifested to Israel, I came baptizing in water." John testified saying, "I have seen **the Spirit** descending as a dove out of heaven, and **He** remained upon Him. I did not recognize Him, but He who sent me to baptize in water said to me, 'He upon whom you see **the Spirit** descending and remaining upon Him, this is the one who baptizes in **the Holy Spirit**.' I myself have seen, and have testified that this is the Son of God." [John 1:31–34]

Summarizing this third pronouncement, John the Baptist's prophecy that Jesus would baptize people with the Holy Spirit was so important, so vitally significant to all of us, that it was recorded in all four gospels. In Matthew, Mark, and Luke, John the Baptist prophesied that Jesus would baptize with the Holy Spirit. In the gospel of John, he quoted God as having said that Jesus would baptize with the Holy Spirit. What does it mean to say that Jesus would baptize with the Holy Spirit? How does this apply to you and me? How can such an event, when we experience it, impact and transform our lives? We will discover answers to those questions in later chapters, but let us look next at the ways the Holy Spirit worked in Jesus' earthly ministry, for they provide patterns for the ways the Holy Spirit works in and through us.

JESUS—ANOINTED, FILLED, AND EMPOWERED BY THE HOLY SPIRIT

6–1

THE RELATIONSHIP BETWEEN JESUS AND THE HOLY SPIRIT

One of the most important characteristics of Jesus' earthly ministry was the extent to which He was led and empowered by the Holy Spirit. The Holy Spirit's presence upon Him was absolutely essential for Him to fulfill the purposes for which God had sent Him. This relationship had been foretold in three highly relevant prophecies from Isaiah:

> 1) **The Spirit of the Lord** will rest on Him,
> The spirit of wisdom and understanding,
> The spirit of counsel and strength,
> The spirit of knowledge and the fear of the Lord. [11:2]
>
> 2) Behold, My Servant, whom I uphold;
> My chosen one in whom My soul delights.
> I have put **My Spirit** upon Him;
> He will bring forth justice to the nations. [42:1]
>
> 3) **The Spirit of the Lord God** is upon me,
> Because the Lord has anointed me
> To bring good news to the afflicted;
> He has sent me to bind up the brokenhearted,
> To proclaim liberty to captives,
> And freedom to prisoners;
> To proclaim the favorable year of the Lord,
> And the day of vengeance of our God;
> To comfort all who mourn…[61:1–2]

Through those prophecies, God revealed that He did not intend for Jesus to minister alone, nor did He intend for Jesus to minister merely through His human knowledge, strength, and abilities. God sent the Holy Spirit to Jesus to be continually with Him as His Helper, Mentor, Encourager, and Friend. They ministered cooperatively, and they were in constant communication. They enjoyed each other's fellowship and friendship. Jesus listened to and followed the Holy Spirit's leading. The Holy Spirit continually anointed, filled, and led Jesus as they ministered together in God's power. God intends that we also be in constant communication with the Holy Spirit, that we follow His leading, and that we minister in full cooperation with Him. One of the purposes of this book is to identify ways that we can do our part to cooperate with the Holy Spirit and thereby achieve the objectives that God has for us.

As part of Jesus' preparation for His earthly ministry, God anointed Him with the Holy Spirit.

> And after being baptized, Jesus came up immediately from the water; and behold, the heavens were opened, and he saw **the Spirit of God** descending as a dove and **lighting on Him**, and behold, a voice out of the heavens said, "This is My beloved Son, in whom I am well-pleased." [Matthew 3:16–17]

That event began the fulfillment of Isaiah 42:1. Witnesses saw the Holy Spirit descend upon Jesus in the form of a dove. They heard God say that He was well-pleased with His Son. That event was so pivotal in Jesus' life and so foundational in preparing Him to minister that it was recorded in all four gospels (see also Mark 1:9–11, Luke 3:21–22, and John 1:32–34).

Luke provided the most detailed account of what happened next, "Jesus, **full of the Holy Spirit**, returned from the Jordan and **was led around by the Spirit** in the wilderness for forty days, being tempted by the devil" (Luke 4:1–2a).

After the Holy Spirit came upon Jesus, Luke described Him as being full of the Holy Spirit. When the Bible describes someone as "filled with the Holy Spirit," this filling prepares and empowers the person for an important ministry task. When the Bible says someone is "full of the Holy Spirit," it is usually describing a person who is leading a life of intimate personal communion with the Holy Spirit and is being continuously led by Him. Both of those descriptions applied to Jesus throughout His earthly ministry.

Next the Holy Spirit led Jesus into the wilderness for a time of training and testing. The Holy Spirit led Jesus in the same ways that He leads people today—sometimes through an inner urging, sometimes through an inner voice, and sometimes through circumstances. Being full of the Holy Spirit and being led by the Holy Spirit enabled Jesus to overcome the devil's temptations described in Luke 4:3-13. In the process of overcoming them, Jesus demonstrated His complete trust in the Father, His absolute obedience to the Father, and His total loyalty to the Father. We, too, should be cultivating trust, obedience, and loyalty to the Father.

Luke's gospel continues, "And Jesus returned to Galilee **in the power of the Spirit,** and news about Him spread through all the surrounding district. And He began teaching in their synagogues and was praised by all" (Luke 4:14–15).

From that time forward, Jesus ministered in the power of the Holy Spirit. This was especially evident when He performed healings and miracles.

Even though Jesus had been conceived by the Holy Spirit and was the Son of God, God did not launch His public ministry until Jesus had first been:

- Anointed with the Holy Spirit
- Filled with the Holy Spirit
- Led by the Holy Spirit
- Empowered by the Holy Spirit

In the following four chapters we will examine those aspects of Jesus' relationship with the Holy Spirit and the ways in which they supply patterns and examples for us.

6–2

JESUS—ANOINTED WITH THE HOLY SPIRIT

We read in earlier chapters about Samuel anointing Saul, and later David, to be king of Israel. The act of anointing was an observable ceremony. By it the person being anointed was ordained for the office or ministry to which God had called him. The Old Testament had a simple procedure for anointing someone: a prophet, acting in obedience to specific instructions from God, poured sacred oil onto the head of the person. The sacred oil, prepared according to the instructions that God gave Moses in Exodus 30:23–25, imparted a distinctive fragrance to the anointed person.

When God anointed Jesus with the Holy Spirit, it was a sovereign and unique event for two reasons. First, it was God Himself, rather than one of His prophets, who anointed Jesus. Second, God did not anoint Jesus with oil, a *symbol* of the Holy Spirit. He anointed Jesus *with* the Holy Spirit. Jesus' anointing was of necessity unique because Jesus and His mission were unique.

JESUS—ANOINTED, FILLED, AND EMPOWERED BY THE HOLY SPIRIT   57

God foretold through Isaiah that He would anoint Jesus with the Holy Spirit:

> **The Spirit of the Lord God** is upon me,
> Because the Lord has anointed me… [Isaiah 61:1a]

Jesus' titles of *Christ* and *Messiah* both literally mean "Anointed One." The New Testament was written in Greek and frequently uses the Greek word *Christos*, which means "Anointed One, Messiah, Christ."* In the translation that I used during the writing of this book, the word *Christos* is applied uniquely to Jesus. It is translated "Christ" more than five hundred times; "Christ's" eleven times; and "Messiah" four times. Whenever we say the name *Jesus Christ,* we are saying "Jesus, the One who was uniquely anointed by God."

There are many references in the Bible to Jesus as the unique Anointed One of God. Two examples from the Psalms are:

> The kings of the earth take their stand,
> And the rulers take counsel together
> Against the Lord and **His Anointed**… [2:2]

> You have loved righteousness, and hated wickedness;
> Therefore **God**, Your God, **has anointed You**
> With the oil of joy above Your fellows. [45:7]

In John's gospel, Andrew proclaimed that Jesus was the Messiah.

> One of the two who heard John [the Baptist] speak and followed Him [Jesus], was Andrew, Simon Peter's brother. He found first his own brother Simon and said to him, "We have found **the Messiah**" (which translated means **Christ**). [1:40–41]

Hebrews 1 applies Psalm 45:7 to Jesus:

> But of the Son He says,
> "Your throne, O God, is forever and ever,
> And the righteous scepter is the scepter of His kingdom.
> You have loved righteousness and hated lawlessness;
> Therefore **God**, Your God, **has anointed You**

---

* Babylon Ltd, *Christos.*

With the oil of gladness above Your companions." [1:8a, 9]

Peter, addressing Cornelius and his household, told them:

> "You know of Jesus of Nazareth, how **God anointed Him with the Holy Spirit** and with power, and how He went about doing good and healing all who were oppressed by the devil, for God was with Him." [Acts 10:38]

God anointed Jesus with the Holy Spirit, declaring to everyone, everywhere, for all time, that Jesus is the Christ, the Messiah, the Anointed One of God. God still anoints people with the Holy Spirit today. It is always a sovereign act, so we can do nothing to deserve or earn His anointing. But if we truly desire God's anointing, we can strive to live in such a way as to be ready to receive it should He choose to bestow it upon us.

6–3

JESUS — FILLED WITH THE HOLY SPIRIT

L uke 4 begins this way, "Jesus, **full of the Holy Spirit**…" (Luke 4:1a). Whereas being anointed is an *external* act, being filled with the Holy Spirit is *internal*. It prepares the person for an important ministry opportunity. Throughout His earthly ministry, Jesus was continuously filled with the Holy Spirit. Every element of His being was saturated with the presence of the Holy Spirit. There weren't any voids, empty places, or reserved or off-limit areas that were not filled with the Holy Spirit. He was so thoroughly and completely filled with the Holy Spirit that He was truly a temple in which the Holy Spirit dwelled.

Because Jesus was continuously filled with the Holy Spirit, He was always prepared to minister to people's needs. For example, let's look together at a single day's events as they are recorded in Luke 4.

> And He came down to Capernaum, a city of Galilee, and He was teaching them on the Sabbath; and they were amazed at His teaching, for His message was with authority. [31-32]

The Bible does not describe Jesus' message, but it could not have been an ordinary teaching, for the people who heard Him were amazed at the authority with which He spoke. His message precipitated a ministry opportunity:

> In the synagogue there was a man possessed by the spirit of an unclean demon, and he cried out with a loud voice, "Let us alone! What business do we have with each other, Jesus of Nazareth? Have You come to destroy us? I know who You are—the Holy One of God!" But Jesus rebuked him, saying, "Be quiet and come out of him!" And when the demon had thrown him down in the midst of the people, he came out of him without doing him any harm. [33–35]

That was the first recorded incident of someone casting out a demon, and it was an astonishing event! No one had ever seen anything like it!

> And amazement came upon them all, and they began talking with one another saying, "What is this message? For with authority and power He commands the unclean spirits, and they come out." And the report about Him was spreading into every locality in the surrounding district. [36–37]

The reports of the things that happened that day began to open doors for Jesus to minister in other nearby towns and villages. But the day was still young!

> Then He got up and left the synagogue, and entered Simon's home. Now Simon's mother-in-law was suffering from a high fever, and they asked Him to help her. And standing over her, He rebuked the fever, and it left her; and she immediately got up and waited on them. [38–39]

When Jesus entered the home to which He had been invited for a meal, there was another ministry opportunity awaiting Him. Simon's mother-in-law was very ill and her family asked Jesus to minister to her. Jesus discerned the cause of her illness, dealt with it swiftly and effectively, and she was restored to health.

> While the sun was setting, all those who had any who were sick with various diseases brought them to Him; and laying His hands on each one of them, He was healing them. Demons also were coming out of many,

shouting, "You are the Son of God!" But rebuking them, He would not allow them to speak, because they knew Him to be the Christ. [40–41]

The multitude of people bringing their sick to Jesus was more than simply a spontaneous act. It had undoubtedly been precipitated by Jesus' message and His demonstration of authority over demonic spirits earlier that day. His ability to help the demon-possessed man led to further opportunities to meet people's urgent spiritual and physical needs. And Jesus, working hand-in-hand with the Holy Spirit, was able to minister to them all. Let us be like Jesus, working hand-in-hand with the Holy Spirit to minister to the needs of hurting people.

6–4

JESUS — LED BY THE HOLY SPIRIT

Jesus, full of the Holy Spirit, returned from the Jordan and **was led around by the Spirit** in the wilderness for forty days, being tempted by the devil. And He ate nothing during those days, and when they had ended, He became hungry. [Luke 4:1–2]

During military boot camp, recruits make the transition from civilian life to military life. Boot camp is intentionally harsh so that the trainees can quickly develop the traits and skills that soldiers must have: being physically tough, obeying orders immediately, ignoring the way they feel, performing their duties to the prescribed standards, being absolutely dependable, and trusting their lives to their leaders.

That forty-day period in the wilderness was Jesus' spiritual boot camp, and it was physically demanding. During that intense one-on-one training and mentoring, Jesus developed and honed His ability to listen to and obey the Holy Spirit's voice and to trust His life and ministry to the Holy Spirit's leadership.

Throughout those forty days, the devil repeatedly tempted Jesus: "Take it easy. You don't have to put up with this kind of treatment. Who does the Holy Spirit think He is, telling You what to do? Why listen to Him? You know as much as He does." You get the picture. They were the same kinds of thoughts with which the devil tempts us when we are being trained and mentored by the Holy Spirit. But Jesus was faithful to His calling, and He submitted to the Holy Spirit's training. Paul described it:

> Have this attitude in yourselves which was also in Christ Jesus, who, although He existed in the form of God, did not regard equality with God a thing to be grasped, but emptied Himself, taking the form of a bondservant, and being made in the likeness of men. Being found in appearance as a man, He humbled Himself by becoming obedient to the point of death, even death on a cross. [Philippians 2:5–8]

When Jesus' training was complete, the devil was allowed to present Him with his most enticing temptations: using the spiritual powers with which He have been entrusted for His personal benefit, becoming famous by performing a display of supernatural power to a large audience, and becoming ruler of the earth without enduring any sacrifice. Jesus successfully resisted each temptation and explained why He chose to do so (read Luke 4:3–13).

During the remainder of Jesus' earthly ministry, the Bible does not specify when Jesus was being led by the Holy Spirit and when He was acting on His own initiative. We can infer that when Jesus did anything which seemed out of the ordinary, or when He did something for the first time, it was because of the Holy Spirit's leading. Here are some examples:

- He announced that He fulfilled Isaiah 61:1–2 in the synagogue in Nazareth (Luke 4:14–21).
- He directed Peter to let down his nets for a miraculous catch of fish (Luke 5:4).
- He called Matthew to be His follower (Luke 5:27).
- He restored a man's withered hand, deliberately doing it in the synagogue on the Sabbath (Luke 6:6–11).
- He traveled to the village of Nain and brought a widow's son back to life (Luke 7:11–15).

If we want to conform to Jesus' example, we too must let the Holy Spirit train us so that we can hear and obey His voice and follow His leading. This is absolutely essential in preparing us for the ministry to which the Lord calls us.

6–5

JESUS—EMPOWERED BY THE HOLY SPIRIT

Jesus, having been anointed, filled, and trained by the Holy Spirit, was now prepared to minister in full cooperation with Him.

> And Jesus returned to Galilee **in the power of the Spirit**, and news about Him spread through all the surrounding district. And He began teaching in their synagogues and was praised by all. [Luke 4:14–15]

When the prophet Micah spoke the following, he was contrasting himself with the false prophets of his day, but he was also prophesying about Jesus:

> On the other hand I am filled with power—
> With **the Spirit of the Lord**—
> And with justice and courage
> To make known to Jacob his rebellious act,
> Even to Israel his sin. [3:8]

That verse describes a prominent and very significant aspect of Jesus: He was empowered by the Holy Spirit. Everything that the Holy Spirit has the ability and the power to do, He could do through Jesus. Whatever Jesus was called upon to do, He could do through the power of the Holy Spirit who was continually with Him.

The Greek word for *power* is *dunamis*. *Dunamis* can be translated as "power, powers, miracles, or miraculous powers."* The following verses refer to the power that was available to Jesus:

> And amazement came upon them all, and they began talking with one another saying, "What is this message? For with authority and **power** He commands the unclean spirits and they come out." [Luke 4:36]

> One day He was teaching; and there were some Pharisees and teachers of the law sitting there, who had come from every village of Galilee and Judea and from Jerusalem; and the **power of the Lord** was present for Him to perform healing. [Luke 5:17]

---

* Babylon Ltd., *Dunamis.*

And all the people were trying to touch Him, for **power** was coming from Him and healing them all. [Luke 6:19]

But Jesus said, "Someone did touch Me, for I was aware that **power** had gone out of Me." [Luke 8:46]

In the same way that the Holy Spirit spent time training Jesus, Jesus spent time training His disciples. When He sent them out to minister, He sent them in the same way that God had sent Him—not to minister alone, and not to minister merely through their human knowledge, strength, and abilities. He sent them out to minister in the power of the Holy Spirit, "And He called the twelve together, and gave them **power** and authority over all the demons, and to heal diseases" (Luke 9:1).

Immediately before Jesus ascended back to heaven to take His place at the right hand of the Father, He told His disciples, "And behold, I am sending forth the promise of My Father upon you; but you are to stay in the city until you are clothed with **power** from on high" (Luke 24:49). Then He promised, "But you will receive **power** when the Holy Spirit has come upon you; and you shall be My witnesses both in Jerusalem, and in all Judea and Samaria, and even to the remotest part of the earth" (Acts 1:8).

God did not intend that Jesus minister alone, nor that Jesus minister solely on the basis of His human knowledge, strength, and abilities. That is why He supplied Jesus with the presence and the power of the Holy Spirit. Jesus does not intend that we minister alone, nor solely on the basis of our human knowledge, strength, and abilities. That is why He supplies us with the presence and the power of the Holy Spirit. I have much more to tell you about that later, but let us look next at the ways Jesus ministered to people, for He is our pattern and example.

Section 7

JESUS' EARTHLY MINISTRY

7–1

HOW JESUS DESCRIBED HIS EARTHLY MINISTRY

Jesus announced that His earthly ministry had begun by reading aloud from Isaiah:

> And He came to Nazareth, where He had been brought up; and as was His custom, He entered the synagogue on the Sabbath and stood up to read. And the book of the prophet Isaiah was handed to Him. And He opened the book, and found the place where it was written,
>
> > **"The Spirit of the Lord** is upon Me,
> > Because He anointed Me to preach the gospel to the poor.
> > He has sent Me to proclaim release to the captives,
> > And recovery of sight to the blind,
> > To set free those who are oppressed,
> > To proclaim the favorable year of the Lord."
>
> And He closed the book, gave it back to the attendant and sat down; and the eyes of all in the synagogue were fixed on Him. And He began to say to them, "Today this Scripture has been fulfilled in your hearing." [Luke 4:16–21]

Thus Jesus confirmed to the people in His hometown synagogue that the Messianic prophecy in Isaiah 61:1–2 was about Him. That prophecy declared that the Spirit of the Lord would be upon Jesus to empower Him to minister in five specific ways:

1) Preaching the gospel to the poor
2) Proclaiming release to the captives
3) Proclaiming recovery of sight to the blind
4) Setting free those who are oppressed
5) Proclaiming the favorable year of the Lord

As we shall see in the following five chapters, each of those ways in which Jesus ministered has both a spiritual and a natural aspect. And each provides us with a pattern and an example for our ministry.

7–2

JESUS — PREACHING THE GOSPEL TO THE POOR

Matthew, describing the early part of Jesus' ministry, wrote, "Jesus was going throughout all Galilee, teaching in their synagogues and proclaiming the gospel of the kingdom..." (4:23a).

The word *gospel* means "good news."* The gospel of the kingdom that Jesus preached can be summarized as follows:

- God rules over an eternal kingdom.
- His kingdom extends throughout heaven.
- God's kingdom was about to make a dramatic entrance into the earth.
- Everyone has a place in God's kingdom if they meet God's conditions and are born into the kingdom by the Holy Spirit.

A Jewish religious leader named Nicodemus came to Jesus one night to find out more about who Jesus was. Jesus told him, "Truly, truly, I say to you, unless one is born again he cannot see the kingdom of God" (John 3:3b).

Thinking only in natural terms, Nicodemus asked how a person could be born again. Jesus answered, "Truly, truly, I say to you, unless one is born of water and **the Spirit**, he cannot enter into the kingdom of God" (John 3:5).

Jesus was explaining to Nicodemus that there are two distinct birth processes. First, we must have a natural birth (be born of water) to become humanly alive and enter this earthly realm. Then we must have a supernatural birth (be born of the Spirit) to become spiritually alive and enter the kingdom of God. Furthermore, the only way to be born into God's kingdom is by the Holy Spirit. That is a very important spiritual truth!

Who are the poor to whom Jesus would preach the gospel of the kingdom of God? In the spiritual sense, they are everyone who has a need of God, and that includes all of us. Jesus' good news is that God's kingdom is accessible, "Blessed are the poor in spirit, for theirs is the kingdom of heaven" (Matthew 5:3).

---

* Babylon, Ltd., *Gospel*.

In the natural sense, we consider people poor when they have material needs or are afflicted in some way. Jesus' good news is that our poverty does not limit God, "Blessed are you who are poor, for yours is the kingdom of God" (Luke 6:20b).

Regardless of our degree of natural or spiritual poverty, Jesus' good news is that the kingdom of God is open to us.

7–3

JESUS — PROCLAIMING RELEASE TO THE CAPTIVES

Who are the captives whom Jesus came to liberate? Let's consider four groups:

1)   Captives to sin
2)   Captives to a demonic power
3)   Captives to an oppressive religion
4)   Captives to the fear of dying

1) CAPTIVES TO SIN

Sin is enticing; if it were not, no one would be tempted to sin. The Apostle John pointed out three major categories of temptation that can lead us to sin.

> Do not love the world nor the things in the world. If anyone loves the world, the love of the Father is not in him. For all that is in the world, **the lust of the flesh** and **the lust of the eyes** and **the boastful pride of life**, is not from the Father, but is from the world. The world is passing away, and also its lusts; but the one who does the will of God lives forever. [1 John 2:15–17]

Temptation and lust occur primarily in our minds, stimulated by our senses. They entice us by offering us advantages over other people, fulfillment of secret desires, position, wealth, power, and fame. But temptation is a liar. It would have us believe that we can be fulfilled when we commit sins, and that there will be no consequences. Although the Bible agrees that there is pleasure in sin *for a season*, we will not, indeed we *cannot*, be fulfilled by anything that sin has to offer. And there *will be* consequences. In fact, the consequences to our character, our loved ones, our career, and the people whom we knowingly or unknowingly influence can be devastating. Remember David's sin with Bathsheba!

James explained how temptation and lust lead us toward committing sins.

> Let no one say when he is tempted, "I am being tempted by God"; for God cannot be tempted by evil, and He Himself does not tempt anyone. But each one is tempted when he is carried away and enticed by his own lust. Then when lust has conceived, it gives birth to sin; and when sin is accomplished, it brings forth death. [1:13–15]

One of the consequences of committing sins is that we can become captive to them. Jesus came both to set us free from captivity to sins and to cleanse us from their stain.

2) Captives to a Demonic Power

The result of serious or continual sins can be that we become the captive of a demonic power. Jesus came to set us free from such captivity. He didn't just proclaim that one day people would be released from their captivity; He released them. Notice how simple it was for Jesus to free someone from demonic captivity:

> And He came down to Capernaum, a city of Galilee, and He was teaching them on the Sabbath; and they were amazed at His teaching, for His message was with authority. In the synagogue there was a man possessed by the spirit of an unclean demon, and he cried out with a loud voice, "Let us alone! What business do we have with each other, Jesus of Nazareth? Have You come to destroy us? I know who You are— the Holy One of God!" But Jesus rebuked him, saying, "Be quiet and come out of him!" And when the demon had thrown him down in the midst of the people, he came out of him without doing him any harm. And amazement came upon them all, and they began talking with one another saying, "What is this message? For with authority and power He commands the unclean spirits, and they come out." [Luke 4:31–36]

The eyewitnesses' amazement confirmed that Jesus had done something that they had never seen, or even heard of, before. No one had ever cast out a demon, for no one since Adam's fall had sufficient authority to do so. But this incident clearly demonstrated that demons are no match for Jesus' authority. He spoke and broke the demon's grip on that man.

Mental and physical illnesses can have natural causes, but they can also be caused by demons. Such was the case of the woman in Luke 13. Again, Jesus did not simply talk about releasing captives: He released them:

> And He was teaching in one of the synagogues on the Sabbath. And there was a woman who for eighteen years had had a sickness caused by a spirit; and she was bent double, and could not straighten up at all. When Jesus saw her, He called her over and said to her, "Woman, you are freed from your sickness." And He laid His hands on her; and immediately she was made erect again and began glorifying God. But the synagogue official, indignant because Jesus had healed on the Sabbath, began saying to the crowd in response, "There are six days in which work should be done; so come during them and get healed, and not on the Sabbath day." But the Lord answered him and said, "You hypocrites, does not each of you on the Sabbath untie his ox or his donkey from the stall and lead him away to water him? And this woman, a daughter of Abraham as she is, whom Satan has bound for eighteen long years, should she not have been released from this bond on the Sabbath day?" [10–16]

That occasion was one of many confrontations between Jesus and religious leaders over Jesus breaking their rules. To paraphrase, the synagogue official said, "You are not allowed to do that because it is not included in our rules of acceptable behavior." Jesus' reply was, "I will not be limited by manmade rules as I minister to people's needs. You need to update and liberalize your rules to allow for acts of mercy and compassion, and to allow God to work freely and unhindered in your midst."

Jesus released Mary Magdalene from demonic captivity. After she was set free, she became His devoted follower and was privileged to be the first person to see Him alive after His resurrection, "Now after He had risen early on the first day of the week, He first appeared to Mary Magdalene, from whom He had cast out seven demons" (Mark 16:9).

How glorious it is when Jesus releases us from demonic captivity! And He even takes the stigma of it away, as He did for Mary Magdalene!

When Jesus set someone free from demonic captivity, He did it through the power of the Holy Spirit. Jesus said:

> "If I by Beelzebul cast out demons, by whom do your sons cast them out? For this reason they will be your judges. But if I cast out demons by **the Spirit of God**, then the kingdom of God has come upon you." [Matthew 12:27–28]

Jesus' demonstrated authority over demons confirmed that God's power is greater than Satan's, as the book of 1 John explains, "The Son of God appeared for this purpose, to destroy the works of the devil" (3:8b).

And Jesus, through the power of the Holy Spirit, still sets people free from demonic captivity!

3) CAPTIVES TO AN OPPRESSIVE RELIGION

Jesus came to set people free from oppressive religions, which included Judaism at the time of Jesus' earthly ministry. His harshest rebukes were never directed to "sinners"; they were directed to the scribes, Pharisees, lawyers, and other religious leaders who had perverted Judaism by their interpretations of the Law, supplemented by their own manmade rules:

> Then Jesus spoke to the crowds and to His disciples, saying: "The scribes and the Pharisees have seated themselves in the chair of Moses; therefore all that they tell you, do and observe, but do not do according to their deeds; for they say things, and do not do them. They tie up heavy burdens, and lay them on men's shoulders, but they themselves are unwilling to move them with so much as a finger." [Matthew 23:1–4]

Jesus continued, "But woe to you, scribes and Pharisees, hypocrites, because you shut off the kingdom of heaven from people; for you do not enter in yourselves, nor do you allow those who are entering to go in" (13).

On another occasion, after rebuking the Pharisees, Jesus turned His attention to the lawyers:

> But He said, "Woe to you lawyers as well! For you weigh men down with burdens hard to bear, while you yourselves will not even touch the burdens with one of your fingers...Woe to you lawyers! For you have taken away the key of knowledge; you yourselves did not enter, and you hindered those who were entering." [Luke 11:46; 52]

Jesus came to release the captives of oppressive religions, then and now.

4) CAPTIVES TO THE FEAR OF DYING

There are many emotional prisoners who are captive to their fear of dying. Jesus came to set them free, too.

> Therefore, since then the children share in flesh and blood, He Himself likewise also partook of the same, that through death He might render powerless him who had the power of death, that is, the devil, and might free those who through fear of death were subject to slavery all their lives. [Hebrews 2:14–15]

> …but now has been revealed by the appearing of our Savior Christ Jesus, who abolished death and brought life and immortality to light through the gospel…[2 Timothy 1:10]

By dying and rising to life again, Jesus demonstrated that He has forever conquered death. No Christian need be held captive by the fear of dying, for Jesus came to set us free from that fear.

It makes absolutely no difference to what we have become captive—a sin, a demonic power, an oppressive religion, the fear of dying, or whatever it may be. Jesus has the power and authority to set us free!

7–4

JESUS — PROCLAIMING RECOVERY OF SIGHT TO THE BLIND

The Bible promised that one day the blind would see: "The Lord opens the eyes of the blind…" (Psalm 146:8a); "On that day…out of their gloom and darkness the eyes of the blind will see…" (Isaiah 29:18); "And I will appoint you…to open blind eyes…" (Isaiah 42:6b-7a).

There is no record in the Old Testament of a blind person being healed. Abraham was not used to heal; nor was Moses, Aaron, Samuel, David, Elijah, Isaiah, or any other Old Testament prophet, priest, or king. So when Jesus healed someone who was blind, it was an event without precedent.

The Holy Spirit was empowering Jesus in a way and to an extent that had never before happened.

If we had watched Jesus as He ministered to the blind, what would we have seen? Often He touched the person to whom He was ministering:

> As Jesus went on from there, two blind men followed Him, crying out, "Have mercy on us, Son of David!" When He entered the house, the blind men came up to Him, and Jesus said to them, "Do you believe that I am able to do this?" They said to Him, "Yes, Lord." Then He touched their eyes, saying, "It shall be done to you according to your faith." And their eyes were opened. [Matthew 9:27–30a]

> And they came to Bethsaida. And they brought a blind man to Jesus, and implored Him to touch him. Taking the blind man by the hand, He brought him out of the village; and after spitting on his eyes and laying His hands on him, He asked him, "Do you see anything?" And he looked up and said, "I see men, for I see them like trees, walking around." Then again He laid His hands upon his eyes; and he looked intently and was restored, and began to see everything clearly. [Mark 8:22–25]

> And as He passed by, He saw a man blind from birth. And His disciples asked Him, "Rabbi, who sinned, this man or his parents, that he would be born blind?" Jesus answered, "It was neither that this man sinned, nor his parents; but it was so that the works of God might be displayed in him."...When He had said this, He spat on the ground, and made clay of the spittle, and applied the clay to his eyes, and said to him, "Go, wash in the pool of Siloam" (which is translated, Sent). So he went away and washed, and came back seeing. [John 9:1–3; 6–7]

On another occasion, Jesus asked the blind man to be specific about his request. Then Jesus granted the man's request, without touching him.

> Then they came to Jericho. And as He was leaving Jericho with His disciples and a large crowd, a blind beggar named Bartimaeus, the son of Timaeus, was sitting by the road. When he heard that it was Jesus the Nazarene, he began to cry out and say, "Jesus, Son of David, have mercy on me!" Many were sternly telling him to be quiet, but he kept crying out all the more, "Son of David, have mercy on me!" And Jesus stopped and said, "Call him here." So they called the blind man, saying to him, "Take courage, stand up! He is calling for you." Throwing aside his cloak, he jumped up and came to Jesus. And answering him, Jesus

said, "What do you want Me to do for you?" And the blind man said to Him, "Rabboni, I want to regain my sight!" And Jesus said to him, "Go; your faith has made you well." Immediately he regained his sight and began following Him on the road. [Mark 10:46–52]

What "magic" happened to cause those miraculous healings? The answer, quite simply, is that it was God's power, administered by the Holy Spirit, as God responded to the person's faith and to Jesus.

But in addition to healing the physically blind, Jesus also came to heal the spiritually blind. Judaism, as it was then being practiced, had blinded people to the truth and the simplicity of God's love and His ways. Jesus characterized many of the leaders of Judaism as blind guides because their distorted teachings and manmade rules kept people from seeing the truth about God's goodness. Jesus sternly rebuked them:

"Woe to you, blind guides, who say, 'Whoever swears by the temple, that is nothing; but whoever swears by the gold of the temple, he is obligated.' You fools and blind men! Which is more important, the gold or the temple that sanctified the gold? And 'Whoever swears by the altar, that is nothing, but whoever swears by the offering on it, he is obligated.' You blind men, which is more important, the offering, or the altar that sanctifies the offering? Therefore, whoever swears by the altar, swears both by the altar and by everything on it. And whoever swears by the temple, swears both by the temple and by Him who dwells within it. And whoever swears by heaven, swears both by the throne of God and by Him who sits upon it.

"Woe to you, scribes and Pharisees, hypocrites! For you tithe mint and dill and cummin, and have neglected the weightier provisions of the law: justice and mercy and faithfulness; but these are the things you should have done without neglecting the others. You blind guides, who strain out a gnat and swallow a camel!

"Woe to you, scribes and Pharisees, hypocrites! For you clean the outside of the cup and of the dish, but inside they are full of robbery and self-indulgence. You blind Pharisee, first clean the inside of the cup and of the dish, so that the outside of it may become clean also." [Matthew 23:16–26]

Perhaps even more significant than restoring sight to the few who were physically blind, Jesus came to give sight to many who are spiritually blind. We are all spiritually blind in one way or another.

7–5

JESUS—SETTING FREE THOSE WHO ARE OPPRESSED

The people of Israel felt oppressed and hopeless under the authority and the heavy taxation of the Roman government. Their hope was that the Messiah would come, overthrow the Romans, and set up His kingdom in Israel. But that was not God's plan. Jesus came as the Messiah, but His purpose was not to inaugurate a new earthly government. His purpose was to change people's hearts and attitudes so that they could be truly free, regardless of the government that had temporal authority over them.

Listen to Jesus in the Sermon on the Mount as He explained proper attitudes toward authority and toward other people so that in our hearts we may be truly free:

> "You have heard that it was said, 'An eye for an eye, and a tooth for a tooth.' But I say to you, do not resist an evil person; but whoever slaps you on your right cheek, turn the other to him also. If anyone wants to sue you and take your shirt, let him have your coat also. Whoever forces you to go one mile, go with him two. Give to him who asks of you, and do not turn away from him who wants to borrow from you.
>
> "You have heard that it was said, 'You shall love your neighbor and hate your enemy.' But I say to you, love your enemies and pray for those who persecute you, so that you may be sons of your Father who is in heaven; for He causes His sun to rise on the evil and the good, and sends rain on the righteous and the unrighteous. For if you love those who love you, what reward do you have? Do not even the tax collectors do the same? If you greet only your brothers, what more are you doing than others? Do not even the Gentiles do the same? Therefore you are to be perfect, as your heavenly Father is perfect." [Matthew 5:38–48]

Do you want to have your attitude changed from that of a victim to that of a victor? Jesus, through the transforming power of the Holy Spirit, can accomplish that in you!

Women had an inferior status in the culture of that day, much as they do in some cultures today. Jesus came to set them free. One notable example was the Samaritan woman whom Jesus met at Jacob's well as described in John 4. Jesus revealed Himself to her as the Messiah for all people, whether male or female. An especially remarkable example was the woman brought to Him in John 8:3-11. She had been caught in the very act of adultery. Instead of supporting the position of the scribes and Pharisees, who wanted to stone her in accordance with the Law, Jesus applied a higher principle: God's mercy. He saved her from death, forgave her sins, and sent her away, a free woman.

The woman in Luke 7:36–50 may have been Mary Magdalene. She was washing His feet with her tears, drying them with her hair, and anointing them with perfume. Moved by her need and by her love, Jesus forgave her sins and gave her His blessing of peace.

Jesus still sets oppressed women free today. In those nations that have a predominately Christian culture, the status of women is usually much higher than it is in those whose culture is dominated by other religions.

7–6

JESUS — PROCLAIMING THE FAVORABLE YEAR OF THE LORD

Genesis 6:8 says that Noah found favor in the eyes of the Lord. 1 Samuel 2:26 says that the boy Samuel was growing in favor with the Lord. David prayed:

> Let the words of my mouth and the meditation of my heart
> Be acceptable in Your sight,
> O Lord, my rock and my Redeemer. [Psalm 19:14]

Being acceptable is synonymous with finding favor, and Acts 7:46 says that David found favor in God's sight. Those examples are among the very few instances in the Old Testament where the Bible says someone found favor with God. In contrast, look at this glorious promise that God made through Isaiah:

> Also the foreigners who join themselves to the Lord,
> To minister to Him, and to love the name of the Lord,
> To be His servants, every one who keeps from profaning the Sabbath
> And holds fast My covenant;

> Even those I will bring to My holy mountain
> And make them joyful in My house of prayer.
> Their burnt offerings and their sacrifices will be acceptable on My
>   altar;
> For My house will be called a house of prayer for all the peoples.
>   [Isaiah 56:6–7]

Jesus came to declare that Isaiah's prophesied time of God's acceptance had arrived. We are living in the favorable year of the Lord! God's arms are open wide, outstretched to welcome and accept us when we turn to Him!

In summary, Jesus described five specific ways that He had been sent to minister. The Holy Spirit was upon Him to empower Him to:

1) Preach the gospel to the poor.
2) Proclaim release to the captives.
3) Proclaim recovery of sight to the blind.
4) Set free those who are oppressed.
5) Proclaim the favorable year of the Lord.

How wonderful of Jesus to do all that for them and for us!

THE PROMISE OF THE HOLY SPIRIT

8–1

THE PROMISE OF THE HOLY SPIRIT

During Old Testament times, the Holy Spirit came upon prophets, and they prophesied. He came upon leaders of Israel, and they led Israel's armies to victory. In the gospels, He came upon Zacharias, Elizabeth, and John the Baptist, and they became the first Spirit-filled family. He came upon Jesus in a most powerful and unprecedented way, equipping Him for His earthly ministry. Yet before the Day of Pentecost, there is no biblical record of His coming upon "ordinary" people.

GOD'S PROMISE THROUGH JOEL

Through the prophet Joel, God promised that an era was coming in which the Holy Spirit would come upon and empower ordinary men and women, people like you and me.

> It will come about after this
> That I will pour out My Spirit on all mankind;
> And your sons and daughters will prophesy,
> Your old men will dream dreams,
> Your young men will see visions.
> Even on the male and female servants
> I will pour out My Spirit in those days... [Joel 2:28–29]

GOD'S PROMISE THROUGH ISAIAH

Through Isaiah, God promised that He would pour out the Holy Spirit freely upon people, and that includes us.

> For I will pour out water on the thirsty land
> And streams on the dry ground;
> I will pour out My Spirit on your offspring
> And My blessings on your descendants; [44:3]

JESUS' PROMISE AT THE FEAST OF TABERNACLES

Standing in the temple during the Feast of Tabernacles, Jesus referred to Isaiah 44:3, saying that an era was coming in which the Holy Spirit would be poured out upon His followers, and we are among His followers:

> Now on the last day, the great day of the feast, Jesus stood and cried out, saying, "If anyone is thirsty, let him come to Me and drink. He who believes in Me, as the Scripture said, From his innermost being will flow rivers of living water." But this **He spoke of the Spirit, whom those who believed in Him were to receive;** for the Spirit was not yet given, because Jesus was not yet glorified. [John 7:37–39]

Both in Isaiah's prophecy and in Jesus' reference to it, water was a symbol of the Holy Spirit. Notice also the close connection between a person's thirst for God and God's response of pouring out the Holy Spirit upon him!

John 7:39 refers to the Holy Spirit being given. This means that the Holy Spirit would work in ways that He had not worked before. First, He would be given so that believers could be born again, born of the Holy Spirit. Second, He would be given so that Jesus could baptize believers with the Holy Spirit. Third, He would be given so that He could fill, empower, and transform Jesus' followers. Jesus is our ultimate example and this is the same pattern that we observed earlier for the way in which the Holy Spirit worked in His life and ministry.

JESUS' ENDORSEMENT OF THE HOLY SPIRIT

Have you ever given an enthusiastic, whole-hearted endorsement of someone whom you believe is truly outstanding? It's a real challenge, isn't it, to find the right words so that your listener will appreciate how outstanding the person is. You want so very much for them to believe you that you put all of your credibility on the line. Perhaps that was how Jesus felt when He said about the Holy Spirit, "If you then, being evil, know how to give good gifts to your children, how much more will your heavenly Father give the Holy Spirit to those who ask Him?" (Luke 11:13).

Rather than trying to explicitly describe just how good the promised Holy Spirit is, Jesus chose to use an analogy. You may remember the structure of analogies from standardized tests that you took in school:

A is to *B* as *C* is to _____.

You fill in the blank with your answer. For example,

Feathers are to a *bird* as *hair* is to a *mammal.*

5 is to *2* as *50* is to *20.*

If we put Luke 11:13 into that structure, Jesus' analogy would read like this:

The *best gift we can give our children* is to *our goodness* as the *promised Holy Spirit* is to *God's goodness.*

Jesus testified that God's gift of the Holy Spirit is as much better than any gift that we could possibly give, as God Himself is better than we are. Let that idea sink in for a moment! That's quite a comparison, isn't it? It qualifies as an enthusiastic, wholehearted endorsement of the Holy Spirit, wouldn't you say? And Jesus also promised that God would give us this gift, if we would only ask Him!

8–2

JESUS' PROMISES AT THE LAST SUPPER

John 14–17 records Jesus' instructions to His disciples on the night before His crucifixion. He knew that He would be returning to heaven very soon to retake His position at the Father's right hand. The time for fulfilling the promise of the Holy Spirit was imminent.

THE HOLY SPIRIT WILL BE A HELPER

Jesus had previously told the disciples some things about the Holy Spirit, but that night He told them many more. The first thing He promised was:

> "**I will ask the Father, and He will give you another Helper, that** He may be with you forever; that **is the Spirit of truth**, whom the world cannot receive, because it does not see Him or know Him, but you know Him because He abides with you and will be in you. I will not leave you as orphans; I will come to you." [John 14:16–18]

The Holy Spirit has been actively at work on earth since the beginning. Jesus was announcing that, upon His return to heaven, the Holy Spirit's role on earth would be greatly expanded. Jesus said that He would ask the Father, and the Father would send the Holy Spirit, emphasizing that both He and the Father were very much in one accord about this.

Jesus referred to the Holy Spirit as the Helper because one of the Holy Spirit's roles is to help us. Jesus called Him "the Spirit of truth," verifying that everything the Holy Spirit says is true. Jesus said that the world (that is, people who have not been born again) cannot know the Holy Spirit and are not consciously aware of His presence. But the exciting news for us as Jesus' followers is that the Holy Spirit abides with us, and we can get to know Him. Then Jesus made another promise: He Himself will come to us through the person of the Holy Spirit.

The Holy Spirit Will Teach

Jesus had taught in synagogues, villages, and outdoor settings. There were no cameras or recorders in those days, and no one was documenting His sermons or His conversations. But people who had not personally seen and heard Him also needed His message. Jesus' strategy was simple: the Holy Spirit would enable His disciples to recall what He had taught.

> "These things I have spoken to you while abiding with you. But the Helper, **the Holy Spirit**, whom the Father will send in My name, **He will teach you all things, and bring to your remembrance all that I said to you**." [John 14:25–26]

And the Holy Spirit did, which explains why the gospels are so accurate, so authentic, so God-breathed, and so life-changing to people who read them with an open heart. Another of the Holy Spirit's roles is to teach us the meaning of what Jesus said. The Holy Spirit in that sense is Jesus' replacement, teaching us as Jesus taught His disciples during His earthly ministry.

THE HOLY SPIRIT WILL WITNESS ABOUT JESUS

Another of the Holy Spirit's functions is to be a witness of who Jesus is, of what He has done, and especially of the way in which He purchased salvation and eternal life for us through His death and resurrection. Note also in the following verse that Jesus again emphasized that He and the Father were jointly sending the Holy Spirit, "When the Helper comes, whom I will send to you from the Father, that is **the Spirit of truth** who proceeds from the Father, He **will testify about Me**..." (John 15:26).

Again Jesus promised that He would send the Holy Spirit, "But I tell you the truth: it is to your advantage that I go away; for if I do not go away, the Helper will not come to you; but if I go, **I will send Him to you**" (John 16:7).

What greater recommendation, what greater endorsement could Jesus have made of the importance of the coming of the Holy Spirit? Having Him here would be better than Jesus being here in person!

THE HOLY SPIRIT WILL CONVICT THE WORLD CONCERNING SIN, RIGHTEOUSNESS, AND JUDGMENT

Jesus described three other functions that the Holy Spirit performs:

> And **He**, when He comes, **will convict the world concerning sin and righteousness and judgment**; concerning sin, because they do not believe in Me; and concerning righteousness, because I go to the Father and you no longer see Me; and concerning judgment, because ruler of this world has been judged. [John 16:8–11]

What did Jesus mean? To answer that, let's look at John 3:18:

> He who believes in Him is not judged; he who does not believe has been judged already, because he has not believed in the name of the only begotten Son of God.

The Holy Spirit convicts people of sin who do not believe in Jesus. Why does He do this? Jesus said that it is because people cannot be saved from sin until they believe in Him. The Holy Spirit convicts people concerning righteousness. He does this because Jesus is with the Father and to go where they are, people must first be clothed with Jesus' righteousness. The Holy Spirit convicts people concerning judgment. He does it because Satan has already been judged, and those who belong to Satan's kingdom will receive a similar judgment. The Holy Spirit performs those functions because it is God's desire, it is His will, that no one be judged, that no one perish, as Jesus said:

> "For God so loved the world, that He gave His only begotten Son, that whoever believes in Him shall not perish, but have eternal life. For God did not send the Son into the world to judge the world, but that the world might be saved through Him." [John 3:16–17]

> "For this is the will of My Father, that everyone who beholds the Son and believes in Him will have eternal life, and I Myself will raise him up on the last day." [John 6:40]

THE HOLY SPIRIT WILL DELIVER MESSAGES TO US FROM JESUS

During the short span of His earthly ministry, Jesus could not teach His followers everything that He wanted them to know. There were still many things that they did not yet have the spiritual foundation or maturity to understand. Jesus also knew that He would have many other followers through the ages who needed to be taught. His solution was that the Holy Spirit would teach His followers about Him and about the things of God:

> "I have many more things to say to you, but you cannot bear them now. But when He, **the Spirit of truth**, comes, He **will guide you into all the truth**; for He will not speak on His own initiative, but whatever He hears, He will speak; and He will disclose to you what is to come. He will glorify Me, for He will take of Mine and will disclose it to you. All things that the Father has are Mine; therefore I said that He takes of Mine and will disclose it to you." [John 16:12–15]

The Holy Spirit fulfilled Jesus' promises as He inspired the writers of the gospels and the New Testament letters. He continues to fulfill Jesus' promises today by helping pastors, teachers, and others minister more effectively and by mentoring us who are Jesus' followers. We shall talk more about these functions of the Holy Spirit in later chapters.

8–3

JESUS' INSTRUCTIONS AFTER HIS RESURRECTION

The Apostle Paul defined the gospel of salvation in this way:

> For I delivered to you as of first importance what I also received, that Christ died for our sins according to the Scriptures, and that He was buried, and that He was raised on the third day according to the Scriptures…[1 Corinthians 15:3–4]

When Jesus appeared to His disciples in the Upper Room after His resurrection, they knew with absolute certainty that He had died according to the Scriptures, had been buried, and had risen to life on the third day, for they had witnessed it all. They fulfilled the necessary conditions for salvation. Look what Jesus did: "So Jesus said to them again, 'Peace be with you; as the Father has sent Me, I also send you.' And when He had said this, He breathed on them and said to them, **'Receive the Holy Spirit'**" (John 20:21–22).

When Jesus spoke those words and breathed upon them, they received the Holy Spirit in regeneration. They were born again, born of the Holy Spirit, born into the kingdom of God. But Jesus' command to receive the Holy Spirit also had another meaning. He was commanding them to receive the Holy Spirit *whenever* He came to them and *in whatever way* He came. Jesus was preparing them to receive the Holy Spirit in the way that He would come on the Day of Pentecost!

In His final message to His followers before He returned to heaven, Jesus instructed them again about the promise of the Holy Spirit, "And behold, **I am sending forth the promise of My Father upon you;** but you are to stay in the city until you are clothed with power from on high" (Luke 24:49).

Notice especially Jesus' words "upon you" and "clothed with power." The disciples had already received the Holy Spirit in regeneration, but they had not yet been anointed, filled, and empowered by Him. Acts 1 provides more of Jesus' final message:

> Gathering them together, **He commanded them** not to leave Jerusalem, but **to wait for what the Father had promised,** "Which," He said, "you heard of from Me; for John baptized with water, but **you will be baptized with the Holy Spirit** not many days from now." [Acts 1:4–5]

They asked Him if He was now going to restore the kingdom to Israel, as everyone had been hoping. His response was to refocus them on what He had just said.

> He said to them, "It is not for you to know times or epochs which the Father has fixed by His own authority; but **you will receive power when the Holy Spirit has come upon you;** and you shall be My witnesses both in Jerusalem, and all Judea and Samaria, and even to the remotest part of the earth." [Acts 1:7–8]

Isaiah prophesied of God's promise to pour out the Holy Spirit. So did Joel and so did John the Baptist. Jesus confirmed and reconfirmed the promise that He would baptize believers with the Holy Spirit. The Holy Spirit would then empower them to become effective witnesses throughout the whole world. What an overwhelming promise Jesus gave us! What a magnificent mission He calls us to participate with Him in!

HOLY SPIRIT BAPTISM

9–1

BAPTIZED WITH THE HOLY SPIRIT

An unbelievably exciting era—the era of the church—began on the Day of Pentecost, ushered in by the sound of a mighty rushing wind. Tongues of fire appeared on the heads of the 120 believers who had gathered together in the Upper Room waiting, as Jesus had instructed them, for the promised outpouring of the Holy Spirit. The believers burst forth in spontaneous praise to God, their praises transitioning supernaturally, under the power of the Holy Spirit, into languages that they had never learned. Bystanders from many other countries who were visiting Jerusalem for the Feast of Pentecost were drawn by the sound of the mighty rushing wind. Many of them recognized their own languages being spoken by these disciples. What could all this possibly mean?

But Peter, taking his stand with the eleven, raised his voice and declared to them:

> "Men of Judea, and all you who live in Jerusalem, let this be known to you, and give heed to my words…this is what was spoken of through the prophet Joel:
>
>> 'And it shall be in the last days,' God says,
>> 'That **I will pour forth of My Spirit on all mankind;**
>> And your sons and daughters shall prophesy,
>> And your young men shall see visions,
>> And your old men shall dream dreams;'…Therefore having been exalted to the right hand of God, and having received from the Father **the promise of the Holy Spirit,** He [Jesus] has poured forth this which you both see and hear." [Acts 2:14; 16-17; 33]

The church was born in supernatural power that day! By the end of the day there were, in addition to the 120 who had been in the Upper Room, three thousand more who believed in Jesus, had been baptized with water, and had received God's promise as Jesus baptized them with the Holy Spirit.

9–2

BAPTIZED WITH THE HOLY SPIRIT — NEW TESTAMENT EXPERIENCES

After the Day of Pentecost, did Jesus ever baptize anyone else in the Holy Spirit? Absolutely yes! And that is what we would expect, for Peter's instructions on the Day of Pentecost were:

> "Repent, and each of you be baptized in the name of Jesus Christ for the forgiveness of your sins; and **you will receive the gift of the Holy Spirit. For the promise is for you and your children and for all who are far off, as many as the Lord our God will call to Himself.**" [Acts 2:38–39]

The wonderfully exciting news is that we are all included in "all who are far off, as many as the Lord our God will call to Himself"! Yes, Jesus is still baptizing believers with the Holy Spirit. Let's first look at some other places in Scripture where it happened.

Several years after Pentecost, Stephen was stoned to death (see Acts 7) and a great persecution arose against the church in Jerusalem. In response, the church's mission field expanded as believers scattered throughout the regions of Judea and Samaria, preaching the gospel as they went. Philip began preaching about Christ in the city of Samaria; his ministry included healings, miracles, and casting out demons. During that revival, many people believed in Jesus, were born again, and were baptized in water, but no one was being baptized with the Holy Spirit:

> Now when the apostles in Jerusalem heard that Samaria had received the word of God, they sent them **Peter and John,** who came down and **prayed for them that they might receive the Holy Spirit. For He had not yet fallen upon any of them;** they had simply been baptized in the name of the Lord Jesus. Then **they began laying their hands on them, and they were receiving the Holy Spirit.** [Acts 8:14–17]

The next example is that of Saul of Tarsus, who was actively persecuting believers. Acts 9 describes how he was traveling to Damascus to arrest believers and extradite them to Jerusalem. Jesus suddenly appeared to him on the road, saved him, and called him into the ministry. Saul witnessed about this on many occasions throughout the remainder of his life. Saul was struck temporarily blind, so that his companions had to lead him by the hand to Damascus. After he spent three days fasting and praying, God answered his prayers through an obscure disciple named Ananias.

> And the Lord said to him, "Get up and go to the street called Straight, and inquire at the house of Judas for a man from Tarsus named Saul, for he is praying, and he has seen in a vision a man named Ananias come in and lay his hands on him, so that he may regain his sight." [Acts 9:11–12]

Ananias objected, but the Lord confirmed that this was indeed what He wanted.

> So Ananias departed and entered the house, and after laying his hands on him, said, "Brother Saul, **the Lord Jesus,** who appeared to you on the road by which you were coming, **has sent me so that you may** regain your sight and **be filled with the Holy Spirit.**" And immediately there fell from his eyes something like scales, and he regained his sight, and he got up and was baptized; and he took food and was strengthened.
> Now for several days he was with the disciples who were at Damascus, and immediately he began to proclaim Jesus in the synagogues, saying, "He is the Son of God." [Acts 9:17–20]

Three days after Saul was saved on the Damascus road he was baptized with the Holy Spirit, and he was never the same again. Just as Peter experienced an amazing transformation after he was baptized with the Holy Spirit on the Day of Pentecost, Saul of Tarsus experienced a transformation that astonished those who knew him previously.

About ten years after Pentecost, the Holy Spirit initiated the next major expansion of the church—opening it to the Gentiles. Up until then, all believers were either Jews or converts to Judaism. In Acts 10, an angel appeared to Cornelius, a Roman centurion living in Caesarea. The Bible describes Cornelius as a devout, God-fearing man, a generous man, and a man of prayer. The angel told Cornelius that Peter was staying in Joppa and instructed Cornelius to send some men to bring Peter to his house. Cornelius immediately did as he was told.

Late the following morning, shortly before Cornelius' men arrived, Peter went up on the rooftop to pray while he waited for lunch to be announced.

He fell into a trance and saw a vision, and it was repeated three times. Each time, at the conclusion of the vision, he was told, "What God has cleansed, no longer consider unholy."

> While Peter was reflecting on the vision, **the Spirit said to him,** "Behold, three men are looking for you. But get up, go downstairs and accompany them without misgivings; for I have sent them Myself." [Acts 10:19–20]

The next day, Peter and several of the brethren from Joppa started for Caesarea, arriving the following day. After introductions, Peter told Cornelius and the others gathered there, "I most certainly understand now that God is not one to show partiality, but in every nation the man who fears Him and does what is right, is welcome to Him" (Acts 10:34b-35). Then Peter began preaching about Jesus:

> "You know of Jesus of Nazareth, how God anointed Him with the Holy Spirit and with power, and how He went about doing good and healing all who were oppressed by the devil, for God was with Him." [Acts 10:38]

Peter witnessed to those gathered there that Jesus had been crucified, had been raised from the dead on the third day, and forgives the sins of everyone who believes in Him.

> While Peter was still speaking these words, **the Holy Spirit fell upon all those who were listening to the message.** All the circumcised believers who came with Peter were amazed, because **the gift of the Holy Spirit had been poured out on the Gentiles also. For they were hearing them speaking with tongues and exalting God.** Then Peter answered, "Surely no one can refuse the water for these to be baptized who **received the Holy Spirit just as we did,** can he?" And he ordered them to be baptized in the name of Jesus Christ. [Acts 10:44–48a]

Notice that neither Peter nor any of the brethren with him laid hands on Cornelius or the others gathered there. Nor had Peter told them about his Pentecostal experience. The Holy Spirit sovereignly came upon them just as He had on the Day of Pentecost. They were baptized with the Holy Spirit and began speaking in tongues and praising God, just like the first 120 disciples!

Word quickly spread that Gentiles had received the gospel, and when Peter returned to Jerusalem, he was summoned before the Jewish believers. In his defense, he described what had happened, saying:

> "**The Spirit told me to go** with them without misgivings. These six brethren also went with me and we entered the man's house. And he reported to us how he had seen the angel standing in his house, and saying, 'Send to Joppa and have Simon, who is also called Peter, brought here; and he will speak words to you by which you will be saved, you and all your household.' And as I began to speak, **the Holy Spirit fell upon them** just as He did upon us at the beginning. And **I remembered the word of the Lord, how He used to say, 'John baptized with water, but you will be baptized with the Holy Spirit.'** Therefore if God gave to them the same gift as He gave to us also after believing in the Lord Jesus Christ, who was I that I could stand in God's way?" When they heard this, they quieted down and glorified God, saying, "Well then, God has granted to the Gentiles also the repentance that leads to life." [Acts 11:12–18]

Notice especially Peter's words: that Jesus used to say (implying that Jesus had often said this), "John baptized with water, but you shall be baptized with the Holy Spirit."

Our final example occurred a number of years after this. When Saul of Tarsus, now renamed Paul, first came to Ephesus and met some of the believers, he sensed they were lacking something, and he believed he knew what it was.

> It happened that while Apollos was at Corinth, Paul passed through the upper country and came to Ephesus, and found some disciples. He said to them, **"Did you receive the Holy Spirit when you believed?"** And they said to him, "No, we have not even heard whether there is a Holy Spirit." And he said, "Into what then were you baptized?" And they said, "Into John's baptism." Paul said, "John baptized with the baptism of repentance, telling the people to believe in Him who was coming after him, that is, in Jesus." When they heard this, they were baptized in the name of the Lord Jesus. And when Paul had laid his hands upon them, **the Holy Spirit came on them, and they began speaking with tongues and prophesying.** [Acts 19:1–6]

Notice that these men were already believers, but they were unaware of much that Jesus had made available to them. Paul baptized them with water.

Then he laid his hands on them, and they were baptized with the Holy Spirit. In response, they began speaking in tongues and prophesying.

9–3

BAPTIZED WITH THE HOLY SPIRIT — CONTEMPORARY EXPERIENCES

S ome people assert that the baptism with the Holy Spirit, as well as speaking with tongues, ceased with the death of the original apostles, including Paul. It takes only a single counter-example to disprove that assertion. I will provide two such counter-examples: my wife Brenda and I will describe how it happened to each of us. And there are many other counter-examples that you can seek out for yourself. I have heard that there are an estimated 400 million people living today, all around the world, who can testify to having been baptized with the Holy Spirit.

Brenda and I first visited a Pentecostal church in 1968 at the invitation of Billy Berry, the choir director at the Methodist church in Marietta, Georgia, where we were members. We were in the choir and, knowing how much we both loved inspiring Christian music, Billy said, "Some Sunday night Martha and I need to take you two to Mount Paran Church of God to hear their choir. The music is outstanding, and I believe you'll really enjoy it." Billy was right. The first night we visited, the choir, the soloists, and even the congregational music were wonderful! We enjoyed it all immensely. The rest of the church service, especially the prayer time and the preaching by the pastor, Paul Walker, were much more dynamic and enthusiastic than we were accustomed to, but we enjoyed them as well.

On the way home, Billy gave us a copy of John Sherrill's book *They Speak with Other Tongues*. Neither Brenda nor I knew anything about the baptism with the Holy Spirit or speaking in tongues. In hindsight, that was probably fortunate, for it enabled us to read the book without any biases. I concluded that John Sherrill had investigated the subjects with impartiality, truly seeking to determine if they were authentic and valid. He had interviewed some of the people who later became recognized as pioneers and leaders of the Charismatic movement of the late 1960s and early 1970s. He concluded that the baptism with the Holy Spirit and speaking in tongues are authentic and are valid for today. Near the end of the book, he described his own experience of receiving the baptism with the Holy Spirit and of speaking in tongues after having hands laid on him at a Full Gospel Businessmen's Fellowship International Convention.

I was very impressed both with John Sherrill and with his book. He had investigated the topics in the same way that I would have—methodically and objectively. On the basis of what he wrote, I also concluded that the baptism with the Holy Spirit and speaking with tongues are authentic and valid for today. I decided that I wanted this experience. Brenda read the book, too. She later admitted that my salvation experience had not changed me as much as she believed I needed to be changed. She knew that I needed something more, and she began to pray that somehow I would receive the baptism with the Holy Spirit.

We visited Mount Paran Church of God several more times while we lived in Atlanta. We tried especially to attend their musical specials during the Christmas and Easter seasons. I was disappointed that they did not have an altar call at the end of the services for those desiring the baptism with the Holy Spirit.

I finished graduate school in the fall of 1969 and accepted a job in Orlando, Florida. Paul Walker's father-in-law was the pastor of a Pentecostal church there, and it was one of the first churches we visited. We also visited several other Pentecostal churches. Neither Brenda nor I felt that we would fit in one of them, so we joined a Methodist church. (As an aside, I was raised in an Episcopal church. Brenda was raised in a Southern Baptist church. Neither of us was drawn to the style of the church services of the other's denomination, so while we were dating and after we married, we agreed upon the Methodist church as an acceptable compromise between our two backgrounds.)

Brenda was still secretly praying for me, and I still wanted to be baptized with the Holy Spirit, but I didn't know what to do next. The Pentecostal churches that we visited did not give an altar call for those desiring the baptism with the Holy Spirit. John Sherrill's experience occurred at a Full Gospel Businessmen's Fellowship International Convention, and I didn't know how to find one of those.

I believe it happened during the fall of 1971. Brenda had a prayer partner/friend who attended a Christian retreat led by the Reverend Dennis Bennett, an Episcopal priest who was one of the men mentioned in John Sherrill's book. When Brenda first saw her friend after she returned from the retreat, tears immediately sprang up in her eyes because the change in her friend was so obvious and so dramatic. Her friend had received the baptism with the Holy Spirit! She gave us a copy of Dennis Bennett's book *Nine O'Clock in the Morning*, so named because that is when those first 120 believers were baptized with the Holy Spirit on the Day of Pentecost. The book described the Reverend Bennett's spiritual journey, how he had received the baptism with the Holy Spirit, and the resulting dramatic changes in his life and ministry.

Brenda read the book first. She later admitted that after she read it, she stopped focusing on me and decided that she needed the baptism with the Holy Spirit herself. When she finished reading *Nine O'Clock in the Morning*, she passed it on to me. I can still envision myself in our duplex, lying across our bed reading that book. I was about fifty pages into it when I read something that suddenly gripped me. I felt that this was my time, laid the book down, and prayed to be baptized with the Holy Spirit. I felt very close to the Lord, but nothing "happened." A few nights later, after we had put our infant son to bed, Brenda said she wanted to talk to me about something. I'll let her tell you about it in her own words:

> As a smug, self-righteous Christian, I was frankly disappointed with Gene's salvation experience. Even after turning over his life to Christ, he still had most of the same faults and problems as before! So it was with great interest that I read John Sherrill's book, *They Speak with Other Tongues*. I was relieved to learn about the baptism with the Holy Spirit as a separate experience from salvation. Even though I hadn't learned about it while growing up in the Baptist church, neither had I been taught against it, so I was filled with hope that help was available to meet Gene's needs. I gladly went with him to visit some Pentecostal churches. We also searched the Scriptures and prayed for guidance. Somewhere during this process I completely lost sight of Gene's shortcomings and became painfully aware of my own! I realized that I was self-satisfied and complacent about my own relationship with God. Although I had been born again at the age of seven, all of my doctrines and beliefs had been spoon-fed to me by the pastor of my home church. I decided to lay aside all I had learned and reread the Bible, asking the Lord to teach me Himself. I promised to act on whatever He revealed. It was an intense and exciting experience. For weeks I devoted myself to the Bible with a mounting sense of excitement and anticipation. Wonderfully, I found

that everything I had been taught was true. I also learned that there was more truth revealed in the Bible than I had known before.

My desire was to have a deeper, more vital relationship with God and I was convinced that receiving the baptism with the Holy Spirit, as taught in the New Testament, was indispensable to the process. One fall morning in 1971, I visited a prayer service at a local Episcopal church and requested prayer to receive the baptism with the Holy Spirit. Then I went home and waited expectantly. I believed that I would receive the gift of tongues as a prayer language, but only one word came into my mind as I waited. It was a nonsense word that had been rattling around in my head since childhood. I said it. There were others! Perhaps those many altar calls I had responded to when all I knew to do was to "rededicate my life" were really the Holy Spirit drawing me to be baptized with the Holy Spirit.

The baptism with the Holy Spirit opened the door to a deeper spiritual experience and a closer relationship with the Lord than I had ever known. It was as if I had been turned right-side-up for the first time. The teachings in the Bible suddenly fell into place, and things I had known in my head took root in my heart. Scriptures I had memorized in childhood were easily retrieved and vitally useful for the first time.

Even though praying in tongues is described in 1 Corinthians as the least of the gifts, it was important to me. I had always been good at putting things into words and even began college as a speech major. To be able to yield my well-trained tongue completely to the Spirit's control was the key to opening every other part of me to His control. The stakes are low in yielding your tongue in a private prayer language, because only you and God are involved. All the other spiritual gifts involve other people. It makes sense to start with the least gift. We must crawl before we learn to walk!

As Brenda shared with me what had just happened to her, the only way I can describe what I felt is to say that I began to sense a strange word, definitely not an English word, in my chest. It started with the letter *k* and seemed to consist of about seven letters with three syllables. I somehow knew that I was supposed to raise my arms and hands toward heaven and speak that word, but I certainly was not willing to do that while Brenda was in the room.

Then Brenda said, "Well, I think I'll go take my bath." I thought, "Great! Now is my time," but she didn't go. She thought of some more things to tell me. Again she said, "Well, I think I'll go take my bath." Relieved, I thought that now was the time, but she continued talking. I was thinking, "Please, go take your bath!" Once more she said, "Well, I think I'll go take my bath," and she actually left the room. As soon as she was gone, I rushed out into the backyard, raised my arms and hands toward heaven, and spoke that word. Amazingly, there were more words after that one. I'm not sure how many minutes I stayed out there, rejoicing in the Lord and praising Him in my new language, but it was a novel and glorious experience. And, even more significant, it was the beginning of a new and much deeper relationship with the Lord.

On the Day of Pentecost, as well as at Cornelius' house, those who gathered had a great sense of expectancy, but they did not know what was about to happen. No one laid hands on them or prayed for them, for Jesus Himself sovereignly baptized them with the Holy Spirit. It was the same for me. No one laid hands on me or prayed for me. Jesus sovereignly baptized me with the Holy Spirit. In contrast, the Samaritan believers who were saved under Philip's preaching, as well as the Ephesian believers to whom Paul ministered, were baptized with the Holy Spirit when someone laid hands on them and prayed. And so it was with Brenda. People are still baptized with the Holy Spirit in both ways today—sovereignly by Jesus and in response to the laying on of hands.

INDWELLED AND FILLED WITH THE HOLY SPIRIT

10–1

INDWELLED BY THE HOLY SPIRIT

Many people have the misconception that being indwelled by the Holy Spirit and being filled with the Holy Spirit are synonymous, but they are not. We are indwelled by the Holy Spirit from the time we are born again. It is a permanent condition; He continually dwells within us. He does not leave and return later in response to our behavior, although our behavior may affect our awareness of His presence. He does not depart when we sin and return when we repent, although our sin and repentance can affect our awareness of Him. He does not come to us when we praise and worship God, although our awareness of His presence may be greatly heightened during times of joyous praise or intimate worship. His indwelling is steadfast and constant, for He Himself is the seal that we belong to God, as Paul wrote:

> In Him, you also, after listening to the message of truth, the gospel of your salvation—having also believed, you were sealed in Him with the Holy Spirit of promise, who is given as a pledge of our inheritance. [Ephesians 1:13–14a]

Have you ever considered the almost incomprehensible fact that God, who completely understands us and yet loves us unconditionally, begins dwelling within us when we are born again? Amazing as it may seem, He does, and this was part of His eternal plan. He spoke about it through Ezekiel, announcing that one day the Holy Spirit would dwell within us.

> "Then I will sprinkle clean water on you, and you will be clean; I will cleanse you from all your filthiness and from all your idols. Moreover, I will give you a new heart and put a new spirit within you; and I will remove the heart of stone from your flesh and give you a heart of flesh. And **I will put My Spirit within you** and cause you to walk in My statutes, and you will be careful to observe my ordinances." [36:25–27]

Because God knew that we needed a new heart and a spirit that is alive, He made provision to give them to us. Notice that besides promising to give us new hearts and put the Holy Spirit within us, He explained why these are important. They enable us to know and follow His statutes and ordinances for our own good. He wants us to know and follow them, not from fear or from a sense of duty, but from sincere hearts because we love Him and desire to please Him.

In the next chapter of Ezekiel, God addressed Israel, but His promise was actually to all people everywhere, "**I will put My Spirit within you**, and you will come to life…" (37:14a).

Jesus reiterated the message of Ezekiel's prophecies. He promised that the Holy Spirit would dwell within His followers and would always be available to help them:

> "I will ask the Father, and He will give you another Helper, that He may be with you forever; that is the Spirit of truth, whom the world cannot receive, because it does not see Him or know Him, but you know Him because **He** abides with you, and **will be in you**." [John 14:16–17]

Jesus' promise was not limited to those who were with Him that night in the Upper Room. It is for everyone, everywhere, who believes in Him.

Those prophecies first came to fulfillment on the evening of Jesus' resurrection. The disciples were cowering in a locked room, fearful that they would be arrested and executed, when Jesus appeared and spoke to them:

> So when it was evening on that day, the first day of the week, and when the doors were shut where the disciples were, for fear of the Jews, Jesus came and stood in their midst, and said to them, "Peace be with you." And when He had said this, He showed them both His hands and His side. The disciples then rejoiced when they saw the Lord. So Jesus said to them again, "Peace be with you; as the Father has sent Me, I also send you." And when He had said this, He breathed on them and said to them, **"Receive the Holy Spirit."** [John 20:19–22]

What a life-changing event! They saw the risen Christ! He blessed them and commissioned them! He breathed on them, they were born again in that moment, and the Holy Spirit began to dwell within them! And in the same way that it happened to those early disciples, it happens to us when we believe that Jesus is alive and ask Him to save us. We are born again, the Holy Spirit begins to dwell within us, and we become a temple of God. The Apostle Paul wrote, "Do you not know that you are a temple of God and that the Spirit of God dwells in you?…Or do you not know that your body is a temple of the Holy Spirit who is in you, whom you have from God, and that you are not your own?" (1 Corinthians 3:16; 6:19).

When we are born again, the Holy Spirit begins living within us. He becomes part of us, as Paul wanted us to understand from those two verses.

And something else happens: our ancestry changes and we become children of God.

> For you are all sons of God through faith in Christ Jesus. [Galatians 3:26]

> See how great a love the Father has bestowed upon us, that we would be called children of God; and such we are. [1 John 3:1a]

> The Spirit Himself testifies with our spirit that we are children of God... [Romans 8:16]

We have many chapters to go, and there is good news in every one of them. Read on to learn about the many privileges that God makes available to all of His children!

10–2

FILLED WITH THE HOLY SPIRIT — THE GOSPELS

The indwelling of the Holy Spirit occurs when we are born again, and it is a permanent condition; He continually dwells within us. In contrast, being filled with the Holy Spirit is a transient condition. It occurs to empower us to accomplish an important or urgent ministry task.

A good analogy to being filled with the Holy Spirit is to compare a person to a rechargeable battery and to liken the degree to which they are filled with the Holy Spirit to the amount of charge in the battery. A battery can be fully charged, partially charged, or badly in need of a charge. So it is with being filled by the Holy Spirit.

For biblical examples of people being filled with the Holy Spirit, let's begin with three passages from the early chapters of Luke's gospel. Our first example, which we previously read about, occurred when Mary arrived at Elizabeth's home and Elizabeth was filled with the Holy Spirit:

Now at this time Mary arose and went in a hurry to the hill country, to a city of Judah, and entered the house of Zacharias and greeted Elizabeth. When Elizabeth heard Mary's greeting, the baby leaped in her womb; and Elizabeth was **filled with the Holy Spirit.** And she cried out with a loud voice and said, "Blessed are you among women, and blessed is the fruit of your womb! And how has it happened to me, that the mother of my Lord would come to me? For behold, when the sound of your greeting reached my ears, the baby leaped in my womb for joy. And blessed is she who believed that there would be a fulfillment of what had been spoken to her by the Lord." [Luke 1:39–45]

Why did God fill Elizabeth with the Holy Spirit on that occasion? The answer is: to empower her to bless and encourage Mary. Mary would often remember that blessing and be encouraged. And Elizabeth and Zacharias would often remember it as they were rearing John the Baptist.

The second example is in Luke 1:67, where Zacharias was filled with the Holy Spirit when his son John the Baptist was circumcised and officially given his name. What was God's purpose in filling Zacharias with the Holy Spirit? It was to empower him to prophesy concerning the ministry of his son. That prophecy brought into focus John's mission and their ministry to him as his parents.

And his father Zacharias was **filled with the Holy Spirit,** and prophesied, saying:

"Blessed be the Lord God of Israel,
For He has visited us and accomplished redemption for His
    people,
And has raised up a horn of salvation for us
In the house of David His servant—
As He spoke by the mouth of His holy prophets from of old—
Salvation from our enemies,
And from the hand of all who hate us;
To show mercy toward our fathers,
And to remember His holy covenant,
The oath He swore to Abraham our father,
To grant us that we, being rescued from the hand of our
    enemies,
Might serve Him without fear,
In holiness and righteousness before Him all our days.
And you, child, will be called the prophet of the Most High;

> For you will go on before the Lord to prepare His ways;
> To give to His people the knowledge of salvation
> By the forgiveness of their sins,
> Because of the tender mercy of our God,
> With which the Sunrise from on high will visit us,
> To shine upon those who sit in darkness and the shadow of
>   death,
> To guide our feet into the way of peace." [Luke 1:67–79]

Our third example occurred when Jesus was baptized by John the Baptist and the Holy Spirit descended upon Him in the form of a dove. Luke 4:1 describes Jesus as now being full of the Holy Spirit. And for what purpose? The immediate purpose was to empower Him to overcome Satan's temptations.

> Jesus, **full of the Holy Spirit,** returned from the Jordan and was led around by the Spirit in the wilderness for forty days, being tempted by the devil. And He ate nothing during those days, and when they had ended, He became hungry. And the devil said to Him, "If You are the Son of God, tell this stone to become bread." And Jesus answered him, "It is written, 'Man shall not live on bread alone.'" And he led Him up and showed Him all the kingdoms of the world in a moment of time. And the devil said to Him, "I will give You all this domain and its glory; for it has been handed over to me, and I give it to whomever I wish. Therefore if You worship before me, it shall all be Yours." Jesus answered him, "It is written, 'You shall worship the Lord your God and serve Him only.'"
>
> And he led Him to Jerusalem and had Him stand on the pinnacle of the temple, and said to Him, "If You are the Son of God, throw yourself down from here; for it is written, 'He will command His angels concerning You to guard You,' and, 'On their hands they will bear You up, so that You will not strike Your foot against a stone.'" And Jesus answered and said to him, "It is said, 'You shall not put the Lord your God to the test.'" And when the devil had finished every temptation, he left Him until an opportune time. [Luke 4:1–13]

In those passages, God filled three individuals—Elizabeth, Zacharias, and Jesus—with the Holy Spirit to empower them for an important ministry task. In the same way, God fills us with the Holy Spirit to empower us for important ministry tasks.

10–3

FILLED WITH THE HOLY SPIRIT — THE CHURCH

On the Day of Pentecost, 120 believers were simultaneously filled with the Holy Spirit.

> When the Day of Pentecost had come, they were all together in one place. And suddenly there came from heaven a noise like a violent, rushing wind, and it filled the whole house where they were sitting. And there appeared to them tongues as of fire distributing themselves, and they rested on each one of them. And they were all **filled with the Holy Spirit** and began to speak with other tongues, as the Spirit was giving them utterance. [Acts 2:1–4]

Those 120 followers of Jesus were baptized with the Holy Spirit while the tongues of fire rested upon them. Almost simultaneously, all were filled with the Holy Spirit. For what purpose? It was to enable them to speak in other tongues or languages, and magnify God, so that they could dynamically and effectively witness of His power and magnificence to the throng that had gathered in Jerusalem for the Feast of Pentecost.

Peter was one of those who were filled with the Holy Spirit that morning. God immediately used Peter to preach about Jesus to the curious who had gathered. By the end of the day, three thousand more people believed in Jesus, and the Holy Spirit had given birth to the church.

After the Day of Pentecost, every person in the New Testament who was described as "filled with the Holy Spirit" had previously been or was simultaneously baptized with the Holy Spirit. For instance, the Holy Spirit, using Peter and John, healed a lame man at the gate of the temple (Acts 3). When a crowd gathered to see the man who had just been miraculously healed, Peter preached to them about Jesus. The immediate result of this was not what Peter and John had expected, for the priests and temple guards arrested them.

> On the next day, their rulers and elders and scribes were gathered together in Jerusalem; and Annas the high priest was there, and Caiaphas and John and Alexander, and all who were of high-priestly descent. When they had placed them in the center, they began to inquire, "By

what power, or in what name, have you done this?" Then Peter, **filled with the Holy Spirit,** said to them, "Rulers and elders of the people, if we are on trial today for a benefit done to a sick man, as to how this man has been made well, let it be known to all of you and to all the people of Israel, that by the name of Jesus Christ the Nazarene, whom you crucified, whom God raised from the dead—by this name this man stands here before you in good health. He is the stone which was rejected by you, the builders, but which became the chief corner stone. And there is salvation in no one else; for there is no other name under heaven that has been given among men by which we must be saved." [Acts 4:5–12]

Notice that Peter, who had been filled with the Holy Spirit on the Day of Pentecost, was again filled with the Holy Spirit. And for what purpose? It enabled him to powerfully witness about Jesus to the entire secular and religious leadership of Israel. What was the result?

Now as they observed the confidence of Peter and John and understood that they were uneducated and untrained men, they were amazed, and began to recognize them as having been with Jesus. And seeing the man who had been healed standing with them, they had nothing to say in reply. [Acts 4:13–14]

After consulting among themselves, the ruling body threatened Peter and John and then released them. When they returned to their companions, they reported what had happened. Then everyone rejoiced greatly, praised God mightily, and prayed for boldness to proclaim the gospel. They also prayed that God would provide healings, signs, and wonders to authenticate His message.

"And now, Lord, take note of their threats, and grant that Your bond-servants may speak Your word with all confidence, while You extend Your hand to heal, and signs and wonders take place through the name of Your holy servant Jesus." And when they had prayed, the place where they had gathered together was shaken, and they were all **filled with the Holy Spirit,** and began to speak the word of God with boldness. [Acts 4:29–31]

Why did God fill them with the Holy Spirit, many of whom had previously been filled on the Day of Pentecost? He had two purposes. The first was to assure them that He was with them and that He was pleased with their bold prayers. The second was to answer those prayers and empower them to proclaim the gospel with boldness. Notice that Peter was filled with the Holy Spirit twice on that same day. The significance of the Bible's reporting of this event is that it clearly demonstrates that, as Christians, we can be filled with the Holy Spirit whenever God chooses, to empower us for important acts of ministry.

Moving forward to Acts 6–7, we see Stephen giving powerful testimony to the Council, which undoubtedly included many of the same men to whom Peter and John had witnessed in Acts 4. By the time Stephen concluded his testimony, the members of the Council were enraged.

> Now when they heard this, they were cut to the quick, and they began gnashing their teeth at him. But **being full of the Holy Spirit,** he [Stephen] gazed intently into heaven and saw the glory of God, and Jesus standing at the right hand of God; and he said, "Behold, I see the heavens opened up and the Son of Man standing at the right hand of God." [Acts 7:54–56]

Stephen was described as being full of the Holy Spirit. And why did God do that? To fortify him with courage, trust, and forgiveness for his executioners as Stephen became the first Christian martyr.

> But they cried out with a loud voice, and covered their ears and rushed at him with one impulse. When they had driven him out of the city, they began stoning him, and the witnesses laid aside their robes at the feet of a young man named Saul. They went on stoning Stephen as he called on the Lord and said, "Lord Jesus, receive my spirit!" Then falling on his knees, he cried out with a loud voice, "Lord, do not hold this sin against them!" Having said this, he fell asleep. [Acts 7:57–60]

In Acts 9, Jesus confronted Saul while he was on the way to Damascus to arrest and extradite Christians who lived there. That was Saul's experience of being born again, to which he gave witness on many occasions. Temporarily blinded, he was led into Damascus where he fasted and prayed for three days. Then the Lord sent an obscure disciple named Ananias to pray for Saul.

> But the Lord said to him [Ananias], "Go, for he [Saul] is a chosen instrument of Mine, to bear my name before the Gentiles and kings and the sons of Israel; for I will show him how much he must suffer for My name's sake." So Ananias departed and entered the house, and after

laying hands on him said, "Brother Saul, the Lord Jesus, who appeared to you on the road by which you were coming, has sent me so that you may regain your sight and **be filled with the Holy Spirit.**" [Acts 9:15–17]

Why did God fill Saul with the Holy Spirit? It was to empower him to witness for Jesus and to help him accept the many sufferings that lay ahead.

It was some years later that Saul undertook his first missionary journey with Barnabas. The first country they visited was Cyprus. While they were witnessing to the Roman proconsul there, a magician named Elymas opposed them.

But Saul, who was also known as Paul, **filled with the Holy Spirit**, fixed his gaze on him [Elymas], and said, "You who are full of all deceit and fraud, you son of the devil, you enemy of all righteousness, will you not cease to make crooked the straight ways of the Lord? Now, behold, the hand of the Lord is upon you, and you will be blind and not see the sun for a time." And immediately a mist and a darkness fell upon him, and he went about seeking those who would lead him by the hand. [Acts 13:9–11]

Why did God fill Paul with the Holy Spirit on that occasion? It was to empower him to pronounce God's judgment upon Elymas, who was trying to prevent the Roman proconsul from believing the gospel and being saved.

The scriptures in this chapter display a striking pattern. In every instance in which someone was filled with the Holy Spirit, it occurred as a sovereign act of God. And on every occasion, it was an empowerment for someone to perform an important ministry task related to spreading the gospel.

10–4

FULL OF THE HOLY SPIRIT

Sometimes when the expression "full of the Holy Spirit" is used in the book of Acts, it has a different meaning than the expression "filled with the Holy Spirit." In those instances, it is used to describe someone whose life was characterized by continual close communion with the Holy Spirit. For example, it is used that way twice in the following passage:

So the twelve summoned the congregation of the disciples and said, "It is not desirable for us to neglect the word of God in order to serve tables. Therefore, brethren, select from among you seven men of good reputation, **full of the Spirit** and of wisdom, whom we may put in charge of this task. But we will devote ourselves to prayer and to the ministry of the word." The statement found approval with the whole congregation; and they chose Stephen, a man **full** of faith and **of the Holy Spirit**, and Philip...[Acts 6:2–5a]

Later in the book of Acts, Barnabas was described as a man full of the Holy Spirit:

...and they sent Barnabas off to Antioch. Then when he arrived and witnessed the grace of God, he rejoiced and began to encourage them all with resolute heart to remain true to the Lord; for he was a good man, and **full of the Holy Spirit** and of faith. [Acts 11:22b-24a]

Perhaps we, too, may be described one day as men and women who are full of the Holy Spirit. It is a worthy goal to pursue.

10–5

BE FILLED WITH THE HOLY SPIRIT

We can find two scriptures that suggest we can be filled with the Holy Spirit as we work in partnership with Him. The first scripture assures us that being filled with the Holy Spirit need not be just a one-time experience, "And the disciples were **continually filled** with joy and **with the Holy Spirit**" (Acts 13:52).

The second scripture encourages us to conduct ourselves in such a way as to enable the Holy Spirit to fill us:

Therefore be careful how you walk, not as unwise men, but as wise, making the most of your time, because the days are evil. So then do not be foolish, but understand what the will of the Lord is. And do not get drunk with wine, for that is dissipation, but **be filled with the Spirit,** speaking to one another in psalms and hymns and spiritual songs, singing and making melody with your heart to the Lord; always giving thanks for all things in the name of our Lord Jesus Christ to God, even the Father; and be subject to one another in the fear of Christ. [Ephesians 5:15–21]

Let us cooperate fully with God, setting our hearts to live by this scripture: **be filled with the Holy Spirit.**

THE HOLY SPIRIT'S POWER

11–1

THE POWER OF THE HOLY SPIRIT— GOD WORKING THROUGH US

The scene was Mount Olivet, just outside of Jerusalem. It was Ascension Day, "So when they had come together, they were asking Him, saying, 'Lord, is it at this time You are restoring the kingdom to Israel?'" (Acts 1:6).

The disciples still did not understand what Jesus had been trying to teach them about the kingdom of God. They still hoped He would set up a literal earthly kingdom in Israel. One day He would, but it was not yet that time. However, it was time for God to fulfill His promise to give the Holy Spirit. It was time for the disciples to be sent forth, empowered by the Holy Spirit, as dynamic witnesses of the resurrection of Jesus and the grace of God.

> He [Jesus] said to them, "It is not for you to know times or epochs which the Father has fixed by His own authority; but **you will receive power when the Holy Spirit has come upon you;** and you shall be My witnesses both in Jerusalem, and in all Judea and Samaria, and even to the remotest part of the earth." [Acts 1:7–8]

This is the same verse that the Lord brought to my mind just before I prayed and asked Him to baptize me with the Holy Spirit. You see, a couple that I knew from college were living in Orlando, and Brenda and I had become good friends with them. I sensed that the wife needed Jesus, especially the joy and peace that He can bring. I had already talked with her once about Jesus, but if anyone's testimony ever fell flat, mine did. I was heartbroken that I had been so totally unable to help her. A few months later, that incident came freshly to my mind while I was reading *Nine O'Clock in the Morning*. In the verses that we just read, Jesus said that we would receive power to be His witnesses when the Holy Spirit comes upon us. I felt a desperate need for power to witness to my friend. My prayer was for Jesus to please baptize me with the Holy Spirit so that I might effectively witness to her. As I shared with you earlier, He baptized me with the Holy Spirit just a few days after my prayer.

A couple of months later, I had another opportunity to witness to her. This time everything was different; this time my witness had power; this time my witness was effective. This time she prayed and received Jesus and was born again. Thank You, Lord, that You love her and saved her, and thank You that you let me participate in what You accomplished.

Beginning on the Day of Pentecost, the Holy Spirit began to minister His power in a new way through those who believed in Jesus. Immediately Peter witnessed in the power of the Holy Spirit, resulting in three thousand people being saved and baptized with the Holy Spirit. By Acts 4, the apostles were witnessing in the power of the Holy Spirit throughout the city of Jerusalem, "And **with great power** the apostles were giving testimony to the resurrection of the Lord Jesus, and abundant grace was upon them all" (Acts 4:33).

Moving forward about ten years, we see that the Holy Spirit arranged for Peter to preach the gospel in the home of Cornelius, a Roman centurion and a Gentile. Peter told the people gathered there:

> "You know of Jesus of Nazareth, how **God anointed Him with the Holy Spirit and with power,** and how He went about doing good and healing all who were oppressed by the devil, for God was with Him." [Acts 10:38]

Jesus is our example for the best way to minister. God wants to minister through us in the same way that He ministered through Jesus. He desires to anoint us with the Holy Spirit and with power for the same reason that He anointed Jesus: so that we may do good in His name. God wants the Holy Spirit to be able to work through us in the same ways He worked through Jesus, including healing people who are oppressed by the devil. And God wants to be continually with us through the Holy Spirit who dwells in us.

11–2

THE POWER OF THE HOLY SPIRIT — ESSENTIAL FOR EVANGELISM

In his letter to the church in Rome, Paul described his ministry in this way:

> For I will not presume to speak of anything except what Christ has accomplished through me, resulting in the obedience of the Gentiles

by word and deed, in the power of signs and wonders, in **the power of the Spirit;** so that from Jerusalem and round about as far as Illyricum **I have fully preached the gospel of Christ.** And thus I aspired to preach the gospel, not where Christ was already named, so that I might not build upon another man's foundations; but as it is written,

> "They who had no news of Him shall see,
> And they who have not heard shall understand."
> [Romans 15:18–21]

In the verses that we just read, Paul characterized his ministry as consisting of preaching Christ and ministering signs and wonders. He accomplished those things through "the power of the Holy Spirit," declaring that he had thereby "fully preached the gospel of Christ." According to Paul, signs and wonders ministered through the power of the Holy Spirit are essential accompaniments to communicating the gospel of Christ effectively. Signs and wonders are especially important when one is trying to reach the unchurched, the sort of people to whom Paul often preached. Signs and wonders are also very important when proclaiming the gospel in regions and cultures where those who are being ministered to have either no knowledge or distorted views of who Jesus is and what He has done.

Why are signs and wonders so important to effective evangelism? Because they authenticate the message that is being preached! Without such authentication, evangelism can easily be reduced to offering intellectual arguments that compare contrasting views of God. When this becomes the basis of preaching, how can someone determine which view is true? Paul understood that preaching the gospel under the anointing of the Holy Spirit, authenticated by signs and wonders, together with demonstrating God's love, is absolutely essential to reaching many who are lost.

The corollary to Romans 15:18–21 is also true: without including signs and wonders, the gospel has not been fully preached. If the gospel has not been fully preached, the inescapable conclusion is that many who might otherwise have believed and received salvation have not. How many people do you suppose die, eternally lost, every day, every month, every year because no one fully preached the gospel to them?

Paul wrote that same message to the church in Corinth:

> And when I came to you, brethren, I did not come with superiority of speech or of wisdom, proclaiming to you the testimony of God. For I determined to know nothing among you except Jesus Christ, and Him

crucified. I was with you in weakness and in fear and in much trem-
bling, and my message and my preaching were not in persuasive words
of wisdom, but in **demonstration of the Spirit and of power,** so that
your faith would not rest on the wisdom of men, but on **the power of
God.** [1 Corinthians 2:1–5]

Paul's preaching was accompanied by demonstrations of the power of the
Holy Spirit. He said that it was important that the hearers' faith be based on
the power of God, not on the strength of his preaching. When he wrote this,
he was referring to the bitter lesson he had learned in Athens. Just before he
went to Corinth for the first time, Paul preached at the Areopagus. In that
sermon recorded in Acts 17:16–34, he used logic and reasoning to preach to
his audience. The result was that only a few believed, and there is no subsequent mention of a church in Athens or of Paul ever revisiting that city.

Later in his letter to the Corinthians, Paul again contrasted mere speech
with preaching that is authenticated by demonstrations of the power of the
Holy Spirit. The context is that he was addressing criticisms of himself made
by some of the members of the Corinthian church, "But I will come to you
soon, if the Lord wills, and I shall find out, not the words of those who are
arrogant but their power. For the kingdom of God does not consist in words
but in **power**" (1 Corinthians 4:19–20).

Paul was saying that anyone can talk; anyone can criticize. The validity of
what they say is found in this: does God authenticate their message as he did
Paul's? We can be certain that messages that God authenticates with signs
and wonders are valid; other messages purported to be from God should be
subjected to more careful scrutiny.

Paul wrote that same message to the church in Thessalonica, "For our
gospel did not come to you in word only, but also **in power and in the Holy
Spirit** and with full conviction..." (1 Thessalonians 1:5a).

And he included it in his letter to the church in Colossae:

We proclaim Him, admonishing every man and teaching every man
with all wisdom, that we may present every man complete in Christ.
For this purpose also I labor, striving according to **His power,** which
mightily works within me. [Colossians 1:28–29]

To summarize, six times within letters to four churches, Paul declared
that the power of the Holy Spirit was an indispensable aspect of his ministry.
Since none of us has yet reached the spiritual stature of the Apostle Paul, the
power of the Holy Spirit is even more indispensable if we are to be effective

in the ministry to which the Lord calls us. Too many people and too many churches have for too long been trying to preach and evangelize apart from the power of the Holy Spirit. The result is that the church has been much less effective than God desires and much less effective than the needs demand.

11–3

THE POWER OF THE HOLY SPIRIT—PAUL'S PRAYERS FOR US

Five of Paul's prayers for us reference the power of the Holy Spirit. They address other matters as well, but for the moment let us focus on their references to the Holy Spirit. In Romans 15, Paul prayed, "Now may the God of hope fill you with all joy and peace in believing, so that you will abound in hope by the **power of the Holy Spirit**" (13).

That prayer focuses on inward issues: joy, peace, and hope. God wants us to be filled with joy and peace and hope as we continue to believe in and trust in Jesus Christ, our Lord and Savior. Those three qualities are not only highly desirable, they are also essential to leading strong, vibrant, and productive lives for Him. Notice that the source of our strength to lead this kind of life is the power of the Holy Spirit.

In his letter to the church in Ephesus, Paul prayed two more prayers for us. In the first one, in Ephesians 1, he prayed:

> For this reason I too, having heard of the faith in the Lord Jesus which exists among you and your love for all the saints, do not cease giving thanks for you, while making mention of you in my prayers; that the God of our Lord Jesus Christ, the Father of glory, may give to you a spirit of wisdom and of revelation in the knowledge of Him. I pray that the eyes of your heart may be enlightened, so that you will know what is the hope of His calling, what are the riches of the glory of His inheritance in the saints, and what is **the surpassing greatness of His power** toward us who believe. These are in accordance with the working of the strength of His might which He brought about in Christ, when He raised Him from the dead and seated Him at His right hand in the heavenly places, far above all rule and authority and power and dominion, and every name that is named, not only in this age but also in the one to come. And He put all things in subjection under His feet, and gave Him

as head over all things to the church, which is His body, the fullness of
Him who fills all in all. [15–23]

The power of the Holy Spirit is the same power that God demonstrated
when He raised Christ from the dead and seated Him at His right hand.
All the power and authority of Satan and his kingdom were arrayed in a
desperate attempt to prevent God from succeeding. But God's power is
immeasurably greater, and it overwhelmed every opposition and fully
accomplished His purpose. None of us will ever have to face that level of
supernatural opposition while we are living our lives or even as we are
conducting God's business. But from Paul's prayer for us, we know that if
we did, God's power would be more than sufficient. God's power has overcome, can overcome, and will overcome all the power of the enemy.

Paul's prayer in Ephesians 3 reads:

> For this reason I bow my knees before the Father, from whom every
> family in heaven and on earth derives its name, that He would grant
> you, according to the riches of His glory, to **be strengthened with
> power through His Spirit** in the inner man, so that Christ may dwell in
> your hearts through faith; and that you, being rooted and grounded in
> love, may be able to comprehend with all the saints what is the breadth
> and length and height and depth, and to know the love of Christ which
> surpasses knowledge, that you may be filled up to all the fullness of
> God. [14–19]

Paul prayed that we would be strengthened inwardly with the power of
the Holy Spirit for two purposes. The first is so that Christ may dwell in
our hearts through faith. In other words, Paul prayed that Christ would be
able to work freely within us to conform us to Himself. The second purpose
is so that we may understand and experience the fullness of Christ's love.
Paul wrote that as we experience Christ's love in all its fullness, we are being
filled with all the fullness of God. He then concluded his prayer in this way:

> Now to Him who is able to do far more abundantly beyond all that we
> ask or think, according to **the power that works within us,** to Him be
> the glory in the church and in Christ Jesus to all generations forever and
> ever. Amen. [Ephesians 3:20–21]

That power that works within us is the power of the Holy Spirit. God,
through the power of the Holy Spirit, is able to do much more in us and for

us and through us than we even know to ask Him for. He is so much more powerful than we could ever imagine! And the Holy Spirit has every bit of that power at His disposal!

Paul prayed for us in Colossians 1:

> For this reason also, since the day we heard of it, we have not ceased to pray for you and to ask that you may be filled with the knowledge of His will in all spiritual wisdom and understanding, so that you may walk in a manner worthy of the Lord, to please Him in all respects, bearing fruit in every good work and increasing in the knowledge of God; strengthened with all **power**, according to His glorious might, for the attaining of all steadfastness and patience; joyously giving thanks to the Father, who has qualified us to share in the inheritance of the saints in light. [9–12]

Paul prayed that we would be strengthened with power, which means receiving the power of the Holy Spirit. Paul's purpose in praying was so that we might be faithful, patient, joyful, and thankful for all that God has done for us. He also prayed that we would know God's will, that we would be fruitful, and that we would walk in ways that are pleasing to God. It is a magnificent prayer, worthy to be adopted as our life scripture.

Paul's fifth prayer is in the form of a blessing:

> To this end also we pray for you always, that our God may count you worthy of your calling, and fulfill every desire for goodness and the work of faith with **power**, so that the name of our Lord Jesus will be glorified in you, and you in Him, according to the grace of our God and the Lord Jesus Christ. [2 Thessalonians 1:11–12]

Paul prayed that God would fulfill every desire of ours to do works of faith by the power of the Holy Spirit. The reason that Paul prayed such a prayer for us is so that Jesus may be glorified in us. This, too, is a wonderful prayer. It is one that we would do well to regularly pray for ourselves and for other Christians.

As we conclude these chapters about the power of the Holy Spirit, consider the following verse which warns us that all power belongs to God. In whatever way God may choose to partner with us to minister in the power of the Holy Spirit, the power is still His power. It all belongs to Him; it never belongs to us, "But we have this treasure in earthen vessels, so that the surpassing greatness of the **power** will be of God and not from ourselves" (2 Corinthians 4:7).

THE WILL OF GOD

12–1

GOD'S WILL—THAT WE HAVE ETERNAL LIFE

To lay the foundation for a most important upcoming topic—being led by the Holy Spirit—let us look together in the next few chapters at an often misunderstood subject: God's will.

"What is God's will for me?" is a question all of us ponder at one time or another. Nevertheless, few of us are ever given the detailed life plan that we would like to have in answer to that question. Later I will explain why this is so, but first let's study some key scriptures that illuminate God's will for us.

Listen to what Jesus said:

> "For I have come down from heaven, not to do My own will, but **the will of Him who sent me.** This is **the will of Him who sent Me,** that of all that He has given Me I lose nothing, but raise it up on the last day. For this is **the will of My Father**, **that everyone** who beholds the Son and believes in Him **will have eternal life,** and I Myself will raise him up on the last day." [John 6:38–40]

From these verses we see that it is God's will that we behold Jesus and understand who He is. It is God's will that we believe in Jesus as the Son of God, the Messiah, and the Savior of all who come to Him for eternal life. It is God's will that we receive eternal life so that Jesus may raise us up on the last day.

To illustrate this truth, Jesus told this parable about sheep:

> "What do you think? If any man has a hundred sheep, and one of them has gone astray, does he not leave the ninety-nine on the mountains and go and search for the one that is straying? If it turns out that he finds it, truly I say to you, he rejoices over it more than over the ninety-nine which have not gone astray. So **it is not the will of your Father** who is in heaven **that one of these little ones perish."** [Matthew 18:12–14]

Who does the one lost sheep in Jesus' parable represent? This sheep represents each of us, and, according to what Jesus said, it is not God's will that any of us perish. Who do the ninety-nine sheep that the shepherd left on the mountains represent? I believe they are the angels in heaven. Jesus left the angels and His place in heaven to come to earth to find us, the lost ones, and lead us back to the Father.

Psalm 40 prophesied that Jesus would come to earth to do God's will.

> Then I said, "Behold, I come;
> In the scroll of the book it is written of me;
> I delight to do **Your will**, O my God;
> Your Law is within my heart." [7–8]

Notice that Jesus was delighted to fulfill God's will and come to earth to seek and save us. He confirmed that in John 4, "Jesus said to them, 'My food is to do **the will of Him who sent Me** and to accomplish His work'" (34).

Jesus received emotional and spiritual nourishment from God as Jesus did God's will. Jesus' obedience was a continual source of strength for Him.

Was it ever difficult for Jesus to do God's will? Yes, at least on one crucial occasion. God's will was for Jesus, as the perfect sinless sacrificial Lamb, to become our Savior through His substitutionary death on the cross. Jesus' death would involve excruciating pain and suffering, along with temporary separation from God. Jesus struggled mightily in prayer in the Garden of Gethsemane to bring His will into alignment with God's will.

> And He withdrew from them about a stone's throw, and He knelt down and began to pray, saying, "Father, if You are willing, remove this cup from Me; yet **not My will, but Yours be done.**" [Luke 22:41–42]

Because Jesus submitted to the Father's will and fulfilled God's plan of salvation, eternal life is available for everyone. If He had not done so, we all would have remained eternally lost, bearing our own sins, and being judged accordingly for them.

12–2

GOD'S WILL—THAT WE BECOME HIS CHILDREN

It is wonderful to have eternal life, but there is more! When we are born again, we become not only members of a group of people who are grateful that they will one day live in heaven, but we also become children of God.

That's right! When we believe in Jesus and are born of the Holy Spirit, God becomes our Father and we become His children.

> But as many as received Him, to them He gave the right **to become children of God,** even to those who believe in His name, who were born, not of blood nor of the will of the flesh nor of **the will** of man, but **of God.** [John 1:12–13]

In fact, God predestined—He determined in advance—that He wanted us to be His children.

> **He predestined us to adoption as sons** through Jesus Christ to Himself, according to the kind intention of **His will,** to the praise of the glory of His grace, which He freely bestowed on us in the Beloved. [Ephesians 1:5–6]

And God doesn't want just a select few children; He wants all of us to become His children! Isn't that good news?

At the same time, we also become Jesus' brothers and sisters. As Jesus said, "For whoever does the will of My Father who is in heaven, he is my brother and sister and mother." (Matthew 12:50).

What a relationship, what a privilege, to be Jesus' brother or sister! And think about this: if I am Jesus' brother, and you are His brother or sister, then it is inescapable that I am your brother and you are my brother or sister. And this relationship will hold throughout all eternity.

12–3

GOD'S WILL—THAT ALL THINGS BE MADE COMPLETE IN CHRIST

Today we are living somewhere in the middle of eternity. Some key events occurred in the distant past that resulted in our having to live in a wounded world. Two of the most significant of those events were the fall of Satan and, later, the fall of Adam and Eve. But things will not always be in the fallen state that they are in today because:

He made known to us the mystery of **His will,** according to His kind intention which He purposed in Him with a view to an administration suitable to the fullness of the times, that is, **the summing up of all things in Christ,** things in the heavens and things upon earth. In Him also we have obtained an inheritance, having been predestined according to His purpose who works all things after the counsel of **His will,** to the end that we who were the first to hope in Christ should be to the praise of His glory. [Ephesians 1:9–12]

There is still much to happen before that day arrives, as Paul described:

For as in Adam all die, so also in Christ shall all be made alive. But each in his own order: Christ the first fruits, after that those who are Christ's at His coming, then comes the end, when He hands over the kingdom to the God and Father, when He has abolished all rule and all authority and power. For He must reign until He has put all His enemies under His feet. The last enemy that will be abolished is death. For He has put all things in subjection under His feet. But when He says, "All things are put in subjection," it is evident that He is excepted who put all things in subjection to Him. When all things are subjected to Him, then the Son Himself also will be subjected to the One who subjected all things to Him, so that God may be all in all. [1 Corinthians 15:22–28]

Following those events, there will be a new heaven and a new earth where we will live forever, as Isaiah 65:17 and 66:22, 2 Peter 3:13, and Revelations 21:1 promise. Won't that be a glorious place to live!

12–4

GOD'S WILL—THAT WE DO WHAT IS RIGHT

The Bible is very clear about God's will for the way we should live. It is God's will that our lives are characterized by continual rejoicing, thankfulness, and prayer, "Rejoice always; pray without ceasing; in everything give thanks; for this is God's will for you in Christ Jesus" (1 Thessalonians 5:16–18).

It is God's will that we submit to our governmental authorities so that we do not bring discredit upon the cause of Christ by displaying a rebellious attitude toward our government.

> Submit yourselves for the Lord's sake to every human institution, whether to a king as the one in authority, or to governors as sent by him for the punishment of evildoers and the praise of those who do right. For such is **the will of God** that by doing right you may silence the ignorance of foolish men. [1 Peter 2:13–15]

It is God's will that we be sexually pure.

> For this is **the will of God,** your sanctification; that is, that you abstain from sexual immorality; that each of you know how to possess his own vessel in sanctification and honor, not in lustful passion, like the Gentiles who do not know God; and that no man transgress and defraud his brother in the matter because the Lord is the avenger in all these things, just as we also told you before and solemnly warned you. For God has not called us for the purpose of impurity, but in sanctification. So, he who rejects this is not rejecting man but the God who gives His Holy Spirit to you. [1 Thessalonians 4:3–8]

We can trust that God will do His part to equip us to live right and conform to His will.

> Now the God of peace, who brought up from the dead the great Shepherd of the sheep through the blood of the eternal covenant, even Jesus our Lord, equip you in every good thing to do **His will,** working in us that which is pleasing in His sight, through Jesus Christ, to whom be the glory forever and ever. Amen. [Hebrews 13:20–21]

God does not promise Christians a life free from suffering. That is not good news, but we must remember that we live in an imperfect world, and suffering will inevitably come to each of us. It may be that we suffer injustices. It may be that we suffer for standing up for what we believe is right or for taking unpopular moral stands, "For it is better, **if God should will it** so, that you suffer for doing what is right rather than for doing what is wrong" (1 Peter 3:17).

It is God's will that, while we are suffering, we do so while fully trusting in Him, "Therefore, **those** also **who suffer according to the will of God** shall entrust their souls to a faithful Creator in doing what is right" (1 Peter 4:19).

It is a privilege to demonstrate our love and respect for God by conforming to His will for us. Let us live as children of God, doing what is right in His eyes. Let us live joyful and thankful lives, trusting in Him regardless of our circumstances.

Section 13

LED BY THE HOLY SPIRIT

13–1

GOD'S PLANS FOR US

O ne of the most encouraging verses in the Bible is this one, "'For I know **the plans that I have for you,'** declares the Lord, '**plans** for welfare and not for calamity to give you a future and a hope'" (Jeremiah 29:11).

Let's consider this verse in the context of God's will. The verse speaks of God's *plans* for us. While God's *will* addresses the desires that He has for us—eternal life, becoming His children, and living moral, upright, joyful, and thankful lives—His *plans* address our major life decisions and our accomplishments. From its context in Jeremiah 29, we see that this verse was contained in a letter that Jeremiah wrote from Jerusalem to the Jewish captives who had been taken to Babylon by King Nebuchadnezzar. The letter began with this prophecy:

> "Thus says the Lord of hosts, the God of Israel, to all the exiles whom I have sent into exile from Jerusalem to Babylon, 'Build houses and live in them; plant gardens and eat their produce. Take wives and become the fathers of sons and daughters, and take wives for your sons and give your daughters to husbands, that they may bear sons and daughters; and multiply there and do not decrease. Seek the welfare of the city where I have sent you into exile, and pray to the Lord on its behalf; for in its welfare you will have welfare.'" [29:4–7]

Through the prophet Jeremiah, God encouraged those Jewish exiles not to withdraw from life, but to live active, fruitful, and productive lives. He encouraged them to build houses, establish businesses, marry, and raise families. But that message was incomplete. What were obviously missing were the details for the ways to accomplish those objectives. Suppose you and I had been among those exiles. We might like to know what sort of house to build. We might want to know the kinds of skills we should learn or the kind of business we should establish. We might like to know whom to marry and perhaps how many children to have, as well as the optimal timing for them. Later we would want to know how best to influence our children's choices of vocations and spouses. Jeremiah's letter does not provide us with the detailed answers that we desire. That raises a very important question: how do we get answers concerning our major life decisions?

Earlier I told you that I would explain why we do not get the detailed answers we hope for when we ask the question, "What is God's will for me?" The reason, quite simply, is that God's *will* addresses the "big picture" issues, the issues we studied in the previous chapters. A better way to phrase our question would be to ask, "What is God's *plan* for my life?" In answer to that question, I have some good news, and I have some bad news. First, let me tell you the good news. We know from Jeremiah 29:11 that God has a plan for each of us, and that it is structured for our ultimate good. This is *very* encouraging!

The bad news is that God seldom reveals detailed information about what our future will bring and when events will happen. Why is that? The short answer is that in making the decisions that can have a major impact on our lives—such as whom to marry or what career to pursue—God wants us to learn to listen to and be guided by the Holy Spirit. The reason is that the Holy Spirit is here with us. He knows the details of God's plans for us, and He can help us follow those plans. Being led by the Holy Spirit, the subject of the next several chapters, is vital if we are to be dynamic, effective Christians.

Let me make one more point as I close this chapter. We are called upon daily to make choices such as what to wear and what to eat for lunch. God's plans do not address minor details such as those; we are free to make whatever choices we prefer.

13–2

LED BY THE HOLY SPIRIT

Jesus is our example for the way to be led by the Holy Spirit. Earlier we observed that Jesus was led by the Holy Spirit from the very beginning of His ministry, "Jesus, full of the Holy Spirit, returned from the Jordan and **was led around by the Spirit** in the wilderness" (Luke 4:1).

Jesus, having just been anointed with the Holy Spirit and being full of the Holy Spirit, began being led by the Holy Spirit, and He fully embraced their relationship. Although He did not always know what situations awaited Him, Jesus fully entrusted Himself to the Father and to the Holy Spirit. The Bible describes His attitude about being led by the Holy Spirit this way:

> Have this attitude in yourselves which was also in Christ Jesus, who, although He existed in the form of God, did not regard equality with God a thing to be grasped, but emptied Himself, taking the form of a bond-servant, and being made in the likeness of men. Being found in appearance as a man, He humbled Himself by becoming obedient to the point of death, even death on a cross. [Philippians 2:5–8]

In the same way that Jesus embraced being led by the Holy Spirit, so can we. In the same way that Jesus fully entrusted Himself to the Father and to the Holy Spirit, so can we.

We learned in the previous chapter that God has an individualized plan for each of us, but He seldom reveals its details to us very far in advance. The *only* way that we can reliably follow His plan for us is to be led by the Holy Spirit. Over the next several chapters, we will study ways that the Holy Spirit led individuals in the early church. Then we will learn practical steps for following the Holy Spirit's leading. After that, we will address ways to consistently listen to the Holy Spirit and follow His leading.

As He was preparing to ascend to heaven, Jesus told His disciples, "But you will receive power when the Holy Spirit has come upon you; and you shall be My witnesses both in Jerusalem, in all Judea and Samaria, and even to the remotest part of the earth" (Acts 1:8).

The remainder of Acts 1 and 2 records the supernatural birth of the church in Jerusalem. Beginning in Acts 3 and continuing into Acts 6, the Bible recounts the church's dynamic growth and ministry in Jerusalem. Beginning in Acts 6 and continuing through Acts 7, the events immediately preceding the martyrdom of Stephen are described.

At that point, the time had arrived for the church to extend beyond Jerusalem and begin ministering throughout Judea and Samaria. The Holy Spirit used Stephen's martyrdom as the trigger event to initiate that:

> Saul was in hearty agreement with putting him [Stephen] to death. And on that day a great persecution began against the church in Jerusalem, and they were all scattered throughout the regions of Judea and Samaria, except the apostles. [Acts 8:1]

That persecution, which appeared to be such a tragedy, was actually part of God's plan. It was the instrument He used to spread the church into Judea and Samaria.

13–3

LED BY THE HOLY SPIRIT — PHILIP

Acts 6:5 introduces Philip as one of the seven original deacons. The Holy Spirit often uses circumstances to direct people, and He used the persecution to get Philip to minister in Samaria:

> Therefore, those who had been scattered went about preaching the word. Philip went down to the city of Samaria and began proclaiming Christ to them. The crowds with one accord were giving attention to what was said by Philip, as they heard and saw the signs which he was performing. For in the case of many who had unclean spirits, they were coming out of them shouting with a loud voice; and many who had been paralyzed and lame were healed. So there was much rejoicing in that city. [Acts 8:4–8]

The Holy Spirit worked mightily through Philip during that revival. People were saved, healed, and set free from evil spirits. No one would voluntarily leave a revival that was as exciting, powerful, and fruitful as that one, certainly not its leader. But there was an important ministry opportunity that could influence an entire nation. The Holy Spirit chose Philip for that assignment and sent an angel to speak to him. "But an angel of the Lord spoke to Philip saying, 'Get up and go south to the road that descends from Jerusalem to Gaza' (This is a desert road)" (Acts 8:26).

God's purpose for that trip was to introduce the gospel into Ethiopia. Philip did not know that, but he obeyed the angel's instructions and departed immediately. From our vantage point we can see how important it was that Philip obey without hesitation, for the opportunity depended upon precise timing:

> So he got up and went; and there was an Ethiopian eunuch, a court official of Candace, queen of the Ethiopians, who was in charge of all her treasure; and he had come to Jerusalem to worship, and he was returning and sitting in his chariot, and was reading the prophet Isaiah. [Acts 8:27–28]

The Holy Spirit had gotten Philip to Samaria by arranging his circumstances. He had directed him to intercept the Ethiopian by sending an angel to speak to him. Now the Holy Spirit Himself spoke to Philip and told him what to do next. "Then **the Spirit said** to Philip, 'Go up and join this chariot'" (Acts 8:29).

Philip did as the Spirit told him. He seized the opportunity and presented the gospel to the Ethiopian official, who believed it and was saved and baptized. Then the Holy Spirit dispatched Philip from there in a most unusual way:

> When they came up out of the water, the Spirit of the Lord snatched Philip away; and the eunuch no longer saw him, but went on his way rejoicing. But Philip found himself at Azotus, and as he passed through he kept preaching the gospel to all the cities until he came to Caesarea. [Acts 8:39-40]

This account of Philip's ministry illustrates some of the diverse methods that the Holy Spirit uses to lead God's people. Let us be open and attentive to Him and respond appropriately to whatever method He may use to lead us.

13–4
LED BY THE HOLY SPIRIT — PETER

Our next example is in Acts 10. While he was in prayer, Peter fell into a trance. Three times he saw a vision of a giant sheet being lowered to the earth, filled with all sorts of animals. The Holy Spirit was using that vision to prepare Peter for his next assignment: to present the gospel to Cornelius, who was a Roman centurion and a Gentile. As soon as the vision ended, messengers from Cornelius arrived and asked for Peter.

> While Peter was reflecting on the vision, **the Spirit said to him,** "Behold, three men are looking for you. But get up, go downstairs, and accompany them without misgivings, for I have sent them Myself." [Acts 10:19–20]

There are four important points for us to notice in these verses and the accompanying text. The first is that it was the Holy Spirit Himself who was orchestrating these events: the angel's visitation to Cornelius, Cornelius' sending messengers to Peter, and Peter's vision. Notice especially the preciseness of the Holy Spirit's timing: Cornelius' messengers arrived just as Peter's vision concluded.

The second point is that the Holy Spirit spoke directly to Peter: "The Spirit said to him." The verse does not explicitly say how He spoke to Peter, but, and this is the third point, Peter immediately recognized that it was the Holy Spirit who was speaking. Peter later testified:

> "And behold, at that moment three men appeared at the house in which we were staying, having been sent to me from Caesarea. **The Spirit told me** to go with them without misgivings. These six brethren also went with me and we entered the man's house." [Acts 11:11–12a]

Peter immediately recognized that it was the Holy Spirit who was speaking to him because this was not the first time that the Holy Spirit had directed Peter.

The fourth point to notice is that both Peter and Cornelius obeyed eagerly and promptly.

A key principle being illustrated here is that God's plans may involve more than a single individual. In this case, although the immediate purpose was to offer salvation to Cornelius and his household, God had a much bigger overall purpose: offering salvation to the Gentiles. The first step in God's plan involved our two primary participants—Peter and Cornelius—along with a supporting cast consisting of Peter's companions, Cornelius's servants, the members of Cornelius's household, and a number of his close friends. None of those participants knew God's purpose or the details of His plan. None of them knew what was about to happen, nor did any of them comprehend the potential of its eternal significance. Nevertheless, the Holy Spirit led Peter and Cornelius, in highly individual ways, to accomplish God's purpose and introduce salvation to the Gentiles. Likewise, we may not know the ultimate purpose of a particular ministry opportunity that the Holy Spirit presents to us. If we are faithful to our task, as Peter was, God's purposes will be accomplished.

13–5

LED BY THE HOLY SPIRIT— PAUL AND BARNABAS

L et us move forward to Acts 13:

> Now there were at Antioch, in the church that was there, prophets and teachers: Barnabas, and Simeon who was called Niger, and Lucius of Cyrene, and Manaen who had been brought up with Herod the tetrarch, and Saul. While they were ministering to the Lord and fasting, **the Holy Spirit said,** "Set apart for Me Barnabas and Saul for **the work to which I have called them.**" Then, when they had fasted and prayed and laid their hands on them, they sent them away. So, being **sent out by the Holy Spirit**…[1–4a]

These men were fasting and ministering to the Lord, so they were serious about listening when the Holy Spirit spoke, "**The Holy Spirit said**…." How did He speak this time? At least some, and perhaps all, of those men were prophets. Most likely it was Simeon, Lucius, or Manaen who heard the Holy Spirit and spoke forth prophetically, "Set apart for Me Barnabas and Saul for the work to which I have called them." The Holy Spirit was commissioning Paul and Barnabas's first missionary journey, a journey in which they would establish churches in a number of cities in Asia Minor where the gospel had not previously been preached.

As with Paul and Barnabas, the Holy Spirit may speak to us through some other person. Let us be attentive to Him when He speaks.

13–6

LED BY THE HOLY SPIRIT— THE JERUSALEM COUNCIL

T he next important example is described in Acts 15. A doctrinal dispute had arisen: did Gentile believers need to be circumcised and to keep the Law of Moses? A committee consisting of Paul, Barnabas, and several others from the church in Antioch traveled to Jerusalem to seek a ruling from the apostles and elders there. After the church council reached its decision, they wrote a letter to the church in Antioch, saying:

> For it seemed good to **the Holy Spirit** and to us to lay upon you no greater burden than these essentials: that you abstain from things sacrificed to idols and from blood and from things strangled and from fornication; if you keep yourselves free from such things, you will do well. Farewell. [Acts 15:28–29]

The Holy Spirit guided the early church to the correct answer as they sought to establish doctrinal guidelines for the new Gentile believers. The Holy Spirit guides churches today as they struggle to make doctrinal decisions that affect their members.

13–7

LED BY THE HOLY SPIRIT— PAUL, SILAS, AND TIMOTHY

In Acts 16, Paul and Silas departed from Antioch to visit and encourage the believers in the cities where Paul and Barnabas had previously established churches. Near the beginning of their journey, they met Timothy and invited him to join them.

> They passed though the Phrygian and Galatian region, having been **forbidden by the Holy Spirit** to speak the word in Asia; and after they came to Mysia, they were trying to go into Bithynia, and **the Spirit of Jesus did not permit them;** and passing by Mysia, they came down to Troas. A vision appeared to Paul in the night: a man of Macedonia was standing and appealing to him, and saying, "Come over to Macedonia and help us." When he had seen the vision, immediately we sought to go into Macedonia, concluding that God had called us to preach the gospel to them. [Acts 16:6–10]

The Phrygian and Galatian regions where Paul, Silas, and Timothy traveled are in the western part of Asia Minor, which is modern-day Turkey. The Holy Spirit's plan was for them not to spend any more time establishing churches in Asia. It was time to introduce the gospel into Europe, so

He forbade them to preach anymore where they were. They traveled west, toward Europe, until they reached the region of Mysia. From there they wanted to travel northeast to Bithynia, which would have been deeper into Asia. Again the Holy Spirit forbade them. Man's plans, even those of a man of the stature of the Apostle Paul, at times may not coincide with God's plans. God retains the right to alter anyone's plans so that He may bring them into alignment with His plans.

Then Paul had a vision of a man in Macedonia beckoning to him. An interesting question to ask is, "Since the Holy Spirit was ready for Paul to begin evangelizing in Europe, couldn't He have just spoken to Paul?" The answer, of course, is, "Yes." Whatever His reason, the Holy Spirit decided to use a vision to speak to Paul this time. Notice that the text says, "We…concluded that…." In following the leading of the Holy Spirit, faith and trust are always required. While it now seemed to our missionaries that the Holy Spirit was leading them to go to Macedonia, they clearly were not absolutely certain. Nevertheless, they started out, remembering that the Holy Spirit had restrained them twice before when they had attempted to go in the wrong direction, and believing that He would restrain them once again if Macedonia was not the right destination.

The continuation of the narrative in Acts 16 is very interesting. They traveled to Philippi, the capitol of Macedonia. As a result of their ministry here, Paul and Silas were arrested, beaten, and thrown into jail. This is a vivid illustration of the way, when we are being led by the Holy Spirit, events may not immediately work out as we expect. But then there was an earthquake, the jailer and his family were saved, Paul and Silas were released, and the church in Philippi was founded. Many years later, the letter that Paul wrote to that church from his prison cell in Rome was included in the New Testament as the much beloved Letter to the Philippians.

This account of Paul and his companions should be especially encouraging to us because it addresses the concerns we might have when we are uncertain if we are really hearing the Holy Spirit. It assures us that He will redirect our paths whenever we stray from God's plans for us if we are attentive to His voice. And He will do it gently and without reproach. What a joy it is to be led by the Holy Spirit!

13–8

THE HOLY SPIRIT — OUR LEADER AND OUR FRIEND

Being led by the Holy Spirit is a voluntary, cooperative relationship both on His part and ours. What an amazing, almost inconceivable privilege it is that the Holy Spirit is willing to lead us. He guides, counsels, and teaches us; we follow, listen, and learn from Him. We are to follow Him and serve Him freely, not through a sense of obligation or an attempt to keep the Law or God's other commandments.

> But now we have been released from the Law, having died to that by which we were bound, so that we serve in newness of the Spirit and not in oldness of the letter. [Romans 7:6]

That is a radical departure from the way many people view God's commandments: they are there, so I must strive to keep them. That is not God's intention. He knows that, of ourselves, we are unable to keep His commandments; they sometimes serve only to show us our shortcomings. So He has provided us a better way. The Holy Spirit helps us do what is pleasing to God, while at the same time helping us to become more and more like Jesus.

Having seen some of the ways that the Holy Spirit led individuals in the early church, let us now turn our attention to His role as our own leader. On the night of the Last Supper, Jesus told His disciples:

> "I will ask the Father, and He will give you another Helper, that He may be with you forever; that is the Spirit of truth, whom the world cannot receive, because it does not see Him or know Him, but you know Him because He abides with you, and will be in you." [John 14:16–17]

A helper in a subordinate relationship is an aide or an assistant. A helper in a peer relationship is an ally or a partner. The Holy Spirit is neither of these. As our Helper in a superior relationship, He is our Leader, hence the phrase, "Led by the Holy Spirit." He is also our Friend. He performs four distinct roles for us:

1)   Advocate
2)   Counselor
3)   Sustainer
4)   Champion

1) OUR ADVOCATE

As our advocate, the Holy Spirit speaks up for us, pleads for us, and inter-cedes for us. He takes our side against the world and against our fiercest enemy, the devil. Jesus said:

> "When they arrest you and hand you over, do not worry beforehand about what you are to say, but say whatever is given you in that hour; for it is not you who speak, but it is the Holy Spirit." [Mark 13:11]

There are many New Testament examples of the Holy Spirit doing that. A few of the most notable include when Jesus was taken before the Sanhedrin, when He was taken before Pontius Pilate, when Peter and John were taken before the Council after healing the lame man, and when Stephen was taken before the Sanhedrin. To the degree that we are being led by the Holy Spirit, we can be confident that He will give us the right words to say when we are called upon to testify. When the Holy Spirit is our advocate, regardless of the outcome, we can be assured that we are representing God faithfully when we deliver His message to our hearers.

2) OUR COUNSELOR

As our Counselor, the Holy Spirit is our Confidant, our Advisor, our Mentor, our Tutor, and our Guide. Jesus said,

> "But when He, the Spirit of truth, comes, He will guide you into all the truth; for He will not speak on His own initiative, but whatever he hears, He will speak; and He will disclose to you what is to come. He will glorify Me, for He will take of Mine and will disclose it to you. All things that the Father has are Mine; therefore I said that He takes of Mine and will disclose it to you." [John 16:13–15]

It is the Holy Spirit's purpose to lead us into all the truth. Perhaps the most important way that He does that is by enlightening Scripture passages to us, showing us what they mean to us and how to apply them in our lives. The

Bible is made of God's words, and God's words are truth, as Jesus affirmed to the Father, "Your word is truth…" (John 17:17b).

It is impossible that God's words should be anything other than the truth. It is important that we understand that the Holy Spirit, who was the author behind the writers of the books of the Bible, will always lead us in accordance with what the Bible says. He will never lead us in ways that are contradictory to the Bible.

3) Our Sustainer

As our Sustainer, the Holy Spirit carries us, upholds us, and comforts us, especially when we are weary or burdened. He strengthens us and provides us with spiritual nourishment, especially when we are weak. He sustains us when we are suffering. He provides us with faith and courage when we face life's trials. He provides us with a way out of or a way through financial difficulties. Whatever comes our way, the Holy Spirit is there to sustain us and uphold us.

4) Our Champion

As our champion, the Holy Spirit is our Patron, our Promoter, our Defender, our Protector, and our intimate Friend. Our fiercest enemies are the devil and his evil spirits, but the Holy Spirit is much more powerful than they, "You are from God, little children, and have overcome them; because greater is He who is in you than he who is in the world" (1 John 4:4).

It is the function of a leader to lead; it is the function of followers to follow. If we are to be led by the Holy Spirit, we must actively cooperate with Him and follow Him. In the next few chapters I will show you some practical steps that we can take to learn how to follow the Holy Spirit.

Section 14

FOLLOWING THE HOLY SPIRIT

HOW TO FOLLOW THE HOLY SPIRIT

Jesus, describing His role as the shepherd of His flock, said:

> "…and **the sheep hear his voice,** and he calls his own sheep by name
> and leads them out. When he puts forth all his own, he goes ahead
> of them, and the sheep follow him because **they know his voice.** A
> stranger they simply will not follow, but will flee from him, because they
> do not know the voice of strangers." [John 10:3b-5]

Later in that passage, He said, "I am the good shepherd, and I know My
own and **My own know Me**" (John 10:14). And again in John 10:27, "My
sheep hear My voice, and I know them, and **they follow Me.**"

The four points that Jesus made about the relationship between the sheep
and the shepherd provide the keys for us to learn how to follow the Holy
Spirit:

1)   Hear His voice
2)   Know His voice
3)   Know Him
4)   Follow Him

We will consider one point per chapter in the next four chapters.

FOLLOWING THE HOLY SPIRIT—HEAR HIS VOICE

It is imperative that we really hear what Jesus says to us. Throughout the
gospels He repeatedly told His followers, "He who has ears to hear, let
him hear."* But Jesus now speaks to us primarily through the Holy Spirit.
Therefore, to hear the things that Jesus wants to tell us, we must listen to the

---

* Matthew 11:15, 13:9, 13:43; Mark 4:9; Luke 8:8, 14:35.

voice of the Holy Spirit. In fact, listening to the Holy Spirit is so important that Jesus said *seven times* in Revelation 2 and 3, "He who has an ear, let him hear what the Spirit says to the churches."*

In a practical sense, what does the voice of the Holy Spirit sound like, and how do we listen to Him? We can find answers to those questions in 1 Kings 19. At this point, Elijah had confronted and killed the prophets of Baal, which caused Jezebel to threaten to kill him. He fled in fear to Mount Sinai, the place where God first spoke to Moses and later gave him the Ten Commandments. Elijah was hiding in a cave there when God spoke to him:

> So He said, "Go forth, and stand on the mountain before the Lord."
> And behold, the Lord was passing by! And a great and strong wind was rending the mountains and breaking in pieces the rocks before the Lord;
> but the Lord was not in the wind. After the wind an earthquake, but the Lord was not in the earthquake. And after the earthquake a fire, but the Lord was not in the fire; and after the fire a sound of a gentle blowing.
> When Elijah heard it, he wrapped his face in his mantle, and went out and stood in the entrance of the cave. And behold, a voice came to him and said, "What are you doing here, Elijah?" [1 Kings 19:11–13]

The Lord did not speak to Elijah by means of the powerful or the dramatic—a wind so strong that it shattered boulders, an earthquake, or a fire. He used those demonstrations of His power to reassure Elijah that, regardless of Elijah's fears, He was still God Almighty. But the prelude to His actually speaking to Elijah was the sound of a gentle blowing. When Elijah heard that sound, he humbled himself, wrapped his face in his mantle, and went forth into the presence of the Lord to hear what He would say.

In the same way God spoke to Elijah, He may choose to use a powerful demonstration or a dramatic event to capture our attention and prepare us to listen to Him. But when He actually speaks to us, it will be in a gentle, quiet voice. We will not be able to hear Him if things around us are noisy. To hear Him speak, we must first tune out the noise and the distractions, perhaps by finding a quiet place where we can be alone with Him.

Likewise, we will not be able to hear Him while we ourselves are speaking, whether in conversation or in prayer. When we have finished expressing to Him the things that are on our hearts—our concerns, our worries, our needs,

---

* 2:7, 11, 17, 29; 3:6, 13, 22.

and our petitions—we must then be quiet and listen for the gentleness of His voice.

I do not know how He speaks to others, but when He speaks to me, it is with an inner voice that is almost like my own thoughts. In my mind I speak to Him, and He responds by speaking within me, speaking to my heart and to my mind. It is in my heart that I recognize that it is He; it is in my mind that I hear what He is saying. Our conversation is not audible; it could not be heard by anyone nearby.

14–3

FOLLOWING THE HOLY SPIRIT—KNOW HIS VOICE

A natural question to ask is: "How can we distinguish when the Holy Spirit is speaking to us?" That is an excellent question, a critically important question, and one definitely not to be addressed lightly. The answer lies in Jesus' second point, "Know His voice." Some years ago, it was common for stand-up comedians to imitate well-known people who had distinctive voices and speaking styles. Some of those who were frequently parodied were John Wayne, Jimmy Stewart, James Cagney, John F. Kennedy, and Richard Nixon. We were entertained with imitations of their speech and mannerisms, but it was never the comedian's intention to convince us that we were actually hearing that person.

We easily recognize the telephone voice of people whom we know well. For instance, I normally recognize my wife's voice after she speaks only one or two words. We can quickly identify people whom we know well because we recognize not only the sound of their voice but also the way they express themselves. Just for fun, one of my friends could disguise his telephone voice, and I would probably not recognize him. However, I do not believe that anyone could imitate the voice of my wife or of one of my close friends so well that I would not soon detect the charade.

Back to our question, "How can we discern when the Holy Spirit is speaking to us and not just our own imagination or even a counterfeiting spirit?" The short answer is that discernment is not easy, initially. Learning to recognize the voice of the Holy Spirit, being able to reliably distinguish

His voice from among the others, requires much effort and hard work in the beginning. We start by submitting the message to a testing process, validating it against what the Bible teaches. The book of 1 John describes a number of such tests. They can help us assess whether or not we have heard from God. Messages from the Holy Spirit will pass those tests. Although not every test applies to everything the Holy Spirit says, what He tells us will never conflict with any of those criteria, for the Holy Spirit Himself is the One who inspired John to write them. Any communication from the Holy Spirit:

- Leads us toward the light, for there is no darkness at all in God (1 John 1:5b).
- Leads us away from sin (1 John 2:1a, 2:15–17).
- Leads us to seek forgiveness and cleansing when we have committed sins (1 John 1:9, 2:1–2).
- Aligns with God's commandments (1 John 2:3–5a).
- Encourages us to respond as Jesus would (1 John 2:5b-6).
- Leads us away from hating and toward loving others (1 John 2:9–11).
- Encourages us to know God better (1 John 2:13–14).
- Is the truth (1 John 2:20–21).
- Will not in any way deny or diminish who Jesus is or what He has done (1 John 2:22–23).

Notice how John summarized his purpose in writing those tests, "These things I have written to you concerning those who are trying to deceive you" (1 John 2:26).

Those who are trying to deceive us, whether intentionally or unintentionally, include other people, our own desires and imagination, and counterfeiting evil spirits. We can apply these tests to anything we hear, whatever the source. The truth from God will pass these tests and will never conflict with any of them. That which is purported to be from God, but is not, will fail one or more of the tests.

The voice that speaks within us in alignment with these tests is the voice of the Holy Spirit. This is the voice we must learn to recognize as being His. At the same time, we must learn to discern and ignore voices that purport to be His, but are not.

14–4

FOLLOWING THE HOLY SPIRIT—KNOW HIM

It is possible to know a lot about someone and yet not really know them. For example, we can stay current with what entertainment celebrities or sports figures do without ever meeting them or knowing them personally. Unfortunately, it is possible—even easy—to do the same thing when we study the Bible. We can learn a lot of information about God the Father, about Jesus, and about the Holy Spirit and yet never meet them or get to know them personally. That may have been what Jesus was warning us about when He said, "You search the Scriptures because you think that in them you have eternal life; it is these that testify about Me; and you are unwilling to come to Me so that you may have life" (John 5:39–40).

On another occasion Jesus also warned:

> "Many will say to Me on that day, 'Lord, Lord, did we not prophesy in Your name, and in Your name cast out demons, and in Your name perform many miracles?' And then I will declare to them, 'I never knew you; depart from Me, you who practice lawlessness.'" [Matthew 7:22–23]

It is important that we get to know the Father, that we get to know Jesus, that we get to know the Holy Spirit, and that we are not satisfied with merely knowing about them. Is it possible to know them personally? The answer is an emphatic yes! In fact, that was one of God's primary purposes in establishing the new covenant, which the writer of Hebrews described by quoting Jeremiah 31:31–34:

> For if that first covenant had been faultless, there would have been no occasion sought for a second. For finding fault with them, He says,
>
>> "Behold, days are coming, says the Lord,
>> When I will effect a new covenant
>> With the house of Israel and with the house of Judah;
>> Not like the covenant which I made with their fathers
>> On the day when I took them by the hand
>> To lead them out of the land of Egypt;
>> For they did not continue in My covenant,

> And I did not care for them, says the Lord.
> For this is the covenant that I will make with the house of Israel
> After those days, says the Lord:
> I will put My laws into their minds,
> And I will write them on their hearts.
> And I will be their God,
> And they shall be My people.
> And they shall not teach everyone his fellow citizen,
> And everyone his brother, saying, 'Know the Lord,'
> **For all will know Me,**
> **From the least to the greatest of them.**
> For I will be merciful to their iniquities,
> And I will remember their sins no more." [Hebrews 8:7–12]

Near the end of that passage, God said, "For all will know Me, from the least to the greatest of them." He was emphasizing that it is His purpose, His intention that we all know Him.

Remember, we are seeking an answer to the question, "How we can know the Holy Spirit?" There is a sense in which, because of their unity, knowing the Father, knowing Jesus, and knowing the Holy Spirit are almost inseparable. Nevertheless, let's consider them individually, beginning with Jesus.

14–5

KNOWING JESUS

Mary, the sister of Martha and Lazarus, provided us with an excellent pattern for the way we can get to know Jesus:

> Now as they were traveling along, He entered a village; and a woman named Martha welcomed Him into her home. She had a sister called Mary, who was seated at the Lord's feet, listening to His word. But Martha was distracted with all her preparations; and she came up to Him, and said, "Lord, do You not care that my sister has left me to do all the serving alone? Then tell her to help me." But the Lord answered and said to her, "Martha, Martha, you are worried and bothered about so many things; but only one thing is necessary, for Mary has chosen the good part, which shall not be taken away from her." [Luke 10:38–42]

There were ample opportunities in that situation for Mary to "do things for Jesus." Instead, she chose to simply be with Him, sitting at His feet and listening to Him. Remember, this was not public ministry for Jesus; this was a visit in a private home. What was Mary really doing, and why did Jesus say she had chosen "the good part"? What Mary was doing was listening to what Jesus was saying *to her*! We learn *about* Jesus as we study *what He said and did*; we get to *know* Him personally as we listen to *what He says to us*! Do you see the difference between those two activities? One leads to knowledge about Jesus, and that is a good thing; but the other leads to friendship and fellowship with Jesus, which are so much better!

Applying Mary's pattern is really as simple as it seems. Here's what to do. Take your Bible to a place where there will not be distractions or interruptions. Pray and ask Jesus to join you there, telling Him that you desire to get to know Him better. I assure you that He will honor your request. Then, begin to read anywhere in the gospels—Matthew, Mark, Luke, John— being alert to see what the passage you are reading might be saying to you. When something in what you are reading seems to really be speaking to you, suddenly makes sense, or "seems to leap off the page at you," pause immediately and think about it. Then paraphrase it back to Jesus, "Do You mean that…?" Now listen in the quietness of your heart and mind for His response.

The more time we spend talking to Jesus and listening to Him, the better we get to know Him. Knowing Jesus was certainly the Apostle Paul's desire, "More than that, I count all things to be loss in view of the surpassing value of **knowing Christ Jesus my Lord**…" (Philippians 3:8a).

Let us make this our desire as well.

14–6

KNOWING THE FATHER

We get to know the Father through knowing Jesus, "And He [Jesus] is the radiance of His [the Father's] glory and the exact representation of His nature…" (Hebrews 1:3a). Jesus said, "…no one knows who the Son is except the Father, and who the Father is except the Son, and anyone to whom the Son wills to reveal Him" (Luke 10:22b). During the Last Supper, Jesus told His disciples, "I am the way, and the truth, and the life; no one comes to the Father, but through Me" (John 14:6). He continued, "If you had known Me, you would have known My Father also; from now on you know Him, and have seen Him." (John 14:7). The disciples obviously did not understand how that could be. "Philip said to Him, 'Lord, show us the Father, and it is enough for us.'" (John 14:8).

Jesus replied:

> "Have I been so long with you, and yet you have not come to know Me, Philip? He who has seen Me has seen the Father; how can you say, 'Show us the Father?' Do you not believe that I am in the Father, and the Father is in Me? The words that I say to you I do not speak on My own initiative, but the Father abiding in Me does His works. Believe Me that I am in the Father, and the Father in Me; otherwise believe because of the works themselves." [John 14:9–11]

Speaking through the prophet Jeremiah, the Lord emphasized the importance of knowing Him:

> Thus says the Lord, "Let not a wise man boast of his wisdom, and let not the mighty man boast of his might, let not a rich man boast of his riches; but **let him who boasts boast of this, that he understands and knows Me,** that I am the Lord who exercises lovingkindness, justice, and righteousness on earth; for I delight in these things," declares the Lord. [Jeremiah 9:23–24]

Isn't that an amazing revelation? God desires that we know Him so well that we could even boast about it!

Shortly before Jesus and His disciples left the Upper Room to go to Gethsemane, Jesus returned to the subject of knowing God the Father.

> Jesus spoke these things; and lifting up His eyes to heaven, He said, "Father, the hour has come; glorify Your Son, that the Son may glorify You, even as You gave Him authority over all flesh, that to all whom You have given Him, He may give eternal life. **This is eternal life, that they may know You, the only true God, and Jesus Christ** whom You have sent." [John 17:1–3]

Isn't that another amazing statement? The whole point of Jesus giving us eternal life—a life that is infinitely long and, indeed, will never end—is so that we may fully know the Father and the Son! Let's commit to maximizing this experience, beginning right now!

14–7

KNOWING THE HOLY SPIRIT

As Jesus continued His discourse to His disciples in John 14, He told them:

> "I will ask the Father, and He will give you another Helper, that He may be with you forever; that is, the Spirit of truth, whom the world cannot receive, because it does not see Him or know Him, but **you know Him because He abides with you** and will be in you." [John 14:16–17]

Jesus told the disciples that the Holy Spirit was abiding with them and therefore they already knew the Holy Spirit. It is unclear how aware the disciples were of the Holy Spirit's presence. Jesus was with them physically. They could see Him with their eyes, hear Him with their ears, and touch Him with their hands. As we already know, the Holy Spirit was wherever Jesus was. It seems improbable that the disciples would be able to distinguish the presence of the Holy Spirit from the presence of Jesus. But that would all change as soon as Jesus returned to heaven!

Notice also that Jesus said the Holy Spirit would soon be in them. The end result would be that their relationship with the Holy Spirit would become even more intimate than their relationship with Jesus had been. Jesus had been *with* them, the Holy Spirit would be *in* them, and that relationship, according to Jesus, would last forever!

Earlier in the evening, Jesus had told His disciples, "Truly, truly, I say to you, he who receives whomever I send receives Me; and he who receives Me receives Him who sent Me" (John 13:20).

We normally apply this verse to Jesus sending us forth to witness to other people, and to whether or not they receive us and accept what we say. However, this verse also very much applies to Jesus' sending the Holy Spirit to us, and whether or not we receive Him and accept what He says! We are to receive the Holy Spirit, the One whom Jesus sent, in the same way that we would receive Jesus, the One who sent Him!

We get to know the Holy Spirit in the same way that we get to know Jesus: getting away from distractions and interruptions, asking Him to make His presence real to us, and telling Him that we desire to get to know Him. He will honor our requests. Next, we open our Bibles to whatever place we desire and begin to read, remembering that He is the author behind every book of the Bible. When the words seem to speak personally to us, we pause and think about them. We paraphrase them back to the Holy Spirit, "Does this mean...?" and listen in the quietness of our hearts and minds for His responses. Then we follow up on whatever He says. The more time we spend with the Holy Spirit in this way, the better we will get to know Him.

The Holy Spirit is another Helper, in the same way that Jesus is a Helper. But the Holy Spirit is more than just *a* Helper; He is *our* Helper. We can seek His help whenever we need it. We simply need to ask Him, as we would ask a good friend: "Holy Spirit, will You please help me...?" We explain to Him what we know and don't know about our problem and then listen for His solution. He may speak the answer into our hearts and minds; He may give us the answers through a spiritual gift such as a word of knowledge or a word of wisdom; He may simply give us a quiet assurance that He will handle the problem for us. Asking Him to help us is another way to get to know Him better. So is asking Him to help other people through us.

14–8

FOLLOW HIM

The fourth point that Jesus made about the way to follow the Holy Spirit was to actually begin to do it. Follow Him!

Jesus' practical four-step process to help us learn to follow the Holy Spirit is based upon an analogy to sheep following their shepherd. It begins with hearing the voice of the Holy Spirit as He speaks to us. Before acting, we verify to the best of our ability that it is His voice that we have heard, and not our own imagination or desire, or a counterfeiting spirit. Then, proceeding in faith, we do what He has asked us to do, thankful for another opportunity to please God while also getting to know the Holy Spirit better.

So remember:

1)   Hear His voice.
2)   Know His voice.
3)   Know Him.
4)   Follow Him.

14–9

WALK IN THE SPIRIT

We just studied four steps for learning *how to* follow the Holy Spirit. In this chapter we will progress to the next level—*continually* following the Holy Spirit. The Bible refers to this as walking in the Spirit. In Romans 8, the Apostle Paul encouraged us to walk in the Spirit: that is, to choose our course of action moment by moment in accordance with the way the Holy Spirit directs us. Paul contrasted walking in the Spirit with walking according to the flesh; that is, acting upon what our senses, desires, appetites, ambitions, fantasies, and passions would have us do. Paul also contrasted walking in the Spirit with trying to live simply by obeying laws, including the Law.

> Therefore there is now no condemnation for those who are in Christ Jesus. For the law of the Spirit of life in Christ Jesus has set you free from the law of sin and death. For what the Law could not do, weak as it was through the flesh, God did: sending His own son in the likeness of sinful flesh and as an offering for sin, He condemned sin in the flesh, so that the requirement of the Law might be fulfilled in us, who do not **walk** according to the flesh but **according to the Spirit.** For those who are according to the flesh set their minds on the things of the flesh, but those who are according to the Spirit, the things of the Spirit. For the mind set on the flesh is death, but the mind set on the Spirit is life and peace, because the mind set on the flesh is hostile toward God; for it does not subject itself to the law of God, for it is not even able to do so, and those who are in the flesh cannot please God.
>
> However, you are not in the flesh but in the Spirit, if indeed the Spirit of God dwells in you. But if anyone does not have the Spirit of Christ, he does not belong to Him. If Christ is in you, though the body is dead because of sin, yet the spirit is alive because of righteousness. But if the Spirit of Him who raised Jesus from the dead dwells in you, He who raised Christ Jesus from the dead will also give life to your mortal bodies through His Spirit who dwells in you.
>
> So then, brethren, we are under obligation, not to the flesh, to live according to the flesh—for if you are living according to the flesh, you must die; but if by the Spirit you are putting to death the deeds of the body, you will live. For all who are being **led by the Spirit of God,** these are sons of God. For you have not received a spirit of slavery leading to

> fear again, but you have received a spirit of adoption as sons by which we cry out, "Abba! Father!" The Spirit Himself testifies with our spirit that we are children of God, and if children, heirs also, heirs of God and fellow heirs with Christ, if indeed we suffer with Him so that we may also be glorified with Him. [Romans 8:1–17]

The first key to properly applying this passage is to focus our thought life accordingly, "For those who are according to the flesh **set their minds** on the things of the flesh, but those who are according to the Spirit, the things of the Spirit" (Romans 8:5).

Basically we must choose between two areas in which to focus our thoughts and set our minds: the things of the flesh and the things of the Spirit. Those choices are mutually exclusive; that is, we cannot do both at the same time. We have to choose one or the other, and each choice has consequences, "For the mind set on the flesh is death, but the mind set on the Spirit is life and peace" (Romans 8:6).

Many people want life and peace, but they search for them in the wrong places— through indulging fleshly desires. The verse is very clear: if we want life and peace, we will find them through walking in the Spirit. Following fleshly desires leads to death, and the next verse explains why: "Because the mind set on the flesh is hostile toward God; for it does not subject itself to the law of God, for it is not even able to do so; and those who are in the flesh cannot please God" (Romans 8:7-8).

Life and peace can come only from God. When our mind-set is hostile to Him, we cut ourselves off from the source of, and therefore the possibility of, life and peace.

The second key to properly applying this passage is to live our lives under the constant leadership of the Spirit of God:

> So then, brethren, we are under obligation, not to the flesh, to live according to the flesh—for if you are living according to the flesh, you must die; but if by the Spirit you are putting to death the deeds of the body, you will live. For all who are being **led by the Spirit of God,** these are sons of God. [Romans 8:12–14]

If we are controlled by our desires, passions, and fantasies, we will live a dead-end life. But if we walk in the Spirit, living lives continually led by Him, we will experience the joys and privileges of being sons and daughters of the Father. God will be our Father in such a real and intimate way that we can come to Him and call Him, "Daddy!"

Paul wrote the same message to the Galatian church, but more succinctly:

> But I say, **walk by the Spirit,** and you will not carry out the desire of the flesh. For the flesh sets its desire against the Spirit, and the Spirit against the flesh; for these are in opposition to one another, so that you may not do the things that you please. But if you are **led by the Spirit**, you are not under the Law. [5:16–18]

In this passage Paul emphasized that being led according to the desires of our flesh and being led by the Holy Spirit are much more than just mutually exclusive. They are in active opposition to one another. We must ignore our fleshly natures if we want to follow the Holy Spirit.

To walk in the Spirit means to live in continual communication and cooperation with Him. It is a life characterized by faith, "For we **walk by faith**, not by sight" (2 Corinthians 5:7). It is a life characterized by love. "…and walk in love…" (Ephesians 5:2a). We must walk in the light, as the Holy Spirit lights our path, "Walk as children of the light" (Ephesians 5:8c). Finally, as Paul exhorted the Galatians, "If we live by the Spirit, let us also **walk by the Spirit**" (Galatians 5:25).

THE GIFTS OF THE HOLY SPIRIT

15–1

GIFTS MEETING A SPECIFIC NEED

Our focus in the previous section was upon getting to know the Holy Spirit personally and learning how to follow Him. This relationship with the Holy Spirit is essential for our lives to be characterized by joy, peace, and divine hope. Let us now shift the focus from ourselves to ministering to the needs and hurts of other people. A proper understanding of the nature and purpose of spiritual gifts is foundational to effective ministry.

Paul began 1 Corinthians 12 by writing, "Now concerning spiritual gifts, brethren, I do not want you to be unaware" (1). Some translations read, "I do not want you to be ignorant." If the Holy Spirit did not want the Corinthian Christians to be ignorant about spiritual gifts, then He does not want us to be ignorant about them either.

What are spiritual gifts? The short answer is that they are supernatural gifts from God to His people, given by the Holy Spirit for a specific situation. The primary passages that address spiritual gifts are 1 Corinthians 12 and 14, beginning with the following:

> Now there are varieties of gifts, but the same Spirit. And there are varieties of ministries, and the same Lord. There are varieties of effects, but the same God who works all things in all persons. But to each one is given the manifestation of the Spirit for the common good. For to one is given the word of wisdom through the Spirit, and to another the word of knowledge according to the same Spirit; to another faith by the same Spirit, and to another gifts of healing by the one Spirit, and to another the effecting of miracles, and to another prophecy, and to another the distinguishing of spirits, and to another various kinds of tongues, and to another the interpretation of tongues. But one and the same Spirit works all these things, distributing to each one individually just as He wills. [12:4–11]

Verse 4 says that there are varieties of gifts, and verses 8 to10 name nine of them. We will be looking at each of them in more detail a little later, but suffice it for the moment to know that each gift addresses a specific human need.

Gifts are presents. They are freely offered to bring pleasure or benefit to the intended recipient. I intentionally said "intended recipient" for two reasons. First, a gift is normally addressed to and intended for a specific person. It is not intended for the first person who might leap forward to grab it. Second, the person for whom the gift is intended must accept it. He or she must become its recipient in order to enjoy its benefits. Spiritual gifts are like that. Each one is a present from God to meet a particular need or to accomplish a specific objective. Lest there be any misunderstanding, spiritual gifts are neither talents nor skills nor abilities that a person may possess. Also, they are initiated by the Holy Spirit, even though the Holy Spirit may use a person to deliver a spiritual gift to another person.

Verses 4, 7, and 11 tell us that it is the Holy Spirit who offers these gifts. This says a lot about Him, for a gift is very much a reflection of the one who gives it. Each time the Holy Spirit gives someone one of these gifts, His purpose is to bring pleasure, blessing, and benefit to or through that person.

Verse 5 says that there are varieties of ministries. Ministries are sacred offices and callings to serve people. This verse means that there are many kinds of sacred offices and callings, each serving people in a distinctive way and meeting different sets of needs. The verse continues by saying that it is Jesus who determines to what kind of ministry each of us is called. Like a spiritual gift, a ministry is offered to a specific person. He or she must accept the calling before being able to function in it. We will discuss ministries in later chapters.

Verse 6 says that there are varieties of effects. The effects are the outcomes that result from receiving a spiritual gift or accepting a ministry. It is God who brings about the effects that He desires in those who accept spiritual gifts and ministries.

God is unseen. An earthly minister is an individual who can be seen and heard, and can represent God to people who need a tangible touch from Him. God uses people to minister to other people. One way He does this is as an instrument of His love. Another way is as a conduit for spiritual gifts. Any Christian can minister God's love. Theoretically, any Christian can be used to deliver spiritual gifts. In practice, however, it is those Christians who have been baptized with the Holy Spirit and are being led by the Holy Spirit who are most often used to minister spiritual gifts. There is a very plausible reason for this. It has nothing to do with exclusivity and little to do with people's level of spirituality. Rather, it has to do primarily with their ability to hear the Holy Spirit, their willingness to be used by Him, and their heart attitude toward the person to whom the ministry is directed. The heart attitude of the person ministering spiritual gifts is what 1 Corinthians 13, taken in context, is all about.

The nine spiritual gifts listed in 1 Corinthians 12:8–10 are usually grouped, for purposes of describing them, into three categories:

1) Information gifts—the word of knowledge, the word of wisdom, and the distinguishing of spirits. They provide supernaturally supplied information to help someone who needs it. It is information that the minister would not other-wise know.
2) Vocal gifts—various kinds of tongues, the interpretation of tongues, and prophecy. These are supernatural messages from God. They normally provide exhortation, encourage-ment, or comfort to the person needing them.
3) Power gifts—faith, gifts of healing, and the effecting of mira-cles. These are manifestations of God's power on behalf of the person being ministered to.

There are common themes running throughout these gifts: they are supernatural, they originate with God, and they are distributed through one person to benefit another person. We need to know about spiritual gifts for two important reasons. The first is so we understand the kinds of supernat-ural help that are available from God for our own needs and for the needs of others. The second is to help others by making ourselves available to God as instruments for delivering His spiritual gifts.

Spiritual gifts are not magic. They are not manufactured, created, owned, or distributed at the discretion of the person through whom they are given. Each spiritual gift (not just each type of gift, but each instance of each gift) originates with God. It is an explicit manifestation of His nature and His love for us. He has not delegated to any person His function of creating these gifts. For instance, there is no one who possesses a bag of gifts of healing that he can distribute at will. That is why a question such as, "If you can heal people, why don't you go empty out the hospitals?" shows a lack of understanding of the way God works.

In the next several chapters we will discuss each of the following nine spiritual gifts and the ways they operate.

Information Gifts

1) Word of knowledge
2) Word of wisdom
3) Distinguishing of spirits

Vocal Gifts

1) Various kinds of tongues
2) Interpretation of tongues
3) Prophecy

Power Gifts

1) Gifts of healing
2) Effecting of miracles
3) Faith

15–2

INFORMATION GIFTS

These gifts supply information supernaturally when it is needed to help someone. They are normally delivered in one of two ways. The first is directly from the Holy Spirit to the mind of the intended recipient. The second is from the Holy Spirit to the mind of another person, who then relays the information to the intended recipient. Let's begin with the word of knowledge.

WORD OF KNOWLEDGE

Have you ever prayed and asked the Lord to help you find your car keys, your purse or billfold, or a lost contact lens, and you suddenly looked up and saw it, or you suddenly knew where to look for it? If so, it was likely because God answered your prayer and gave you a word of knowledge. A word of knowledge is information that you either did not know before or couldn't remember, but that you now know because the Holy Spirit told you. The knowledge does not come to you in a "spooky" way. Very simply, one moment you do not know it, and the next moment you know it.

If you have received a word of knowledge from the Holy Spirit, do you now "have" the gift of knowledge, so that you know all knowledge? Of course not! Will God now "gossip" to you about other people's secrets? Absolutely not! So what happens the next time you need some information that only

God can supply? The answer is that you pray and ask Him. Perhaps the Holy Spirit will again give you a gift of a word of knowledge.

Let's take another example of this gift in operation. Suppose someone comes to you for counseling about a long-standing problem that he or she has been struggling with. Let's say that it is a wife who has an unreasonable fear of crowds. Her husband loves to go to ballgames. She goes with him, but she can never really relax and enjoy the outing because of her fear. As you pray for her, you see a mental image of a small girl being jostled by a crowd and getting separated from her parents. The little girl panics. God has just given you a word of knowledge to benefit the person you are counseling. As you relate your mental image to the woman, she suddenly remembers the incident clearly. She can even feel the panic she had felt. Then you pray for her and ask the Lord to remove the fear, to heal her emotions, and to give her peace. And He does. He has just used you to deliver a word of knowledge, the effect of which was to bring healing to someone whom only He could heal.

In a church service or an evangelistic meeting that is being led by a person who believes in the spiritual gifts and allows the Holy Spirit to operate freely, it is not unusual to hear something like, "The Lord has shown me that there is someone here who has just been diagnosed with…If you will come forward and be prayed for, I believe the Lord will heal you." This, too, is an example of a word of knowledge. It is a wonderful gift, especially when it is ministered with integrity, compassion, humility, and love.

WORD OF WISDOM

A word of wisdom is specific information from God that answers the question, "What should I do?" Have you ever been offered a job with a different company, prayed and asked the Lord what to do, and then known (how you knew, you can't really explain, but you knew that you knew) whether to accept it or not? If so, you likely received a word of wisdom from the Lord.

Does that mean you are now wise? No, it does not. Does it mean that the next time you need to make a decision, you will know the answer? No, but it does mean that you should have learned something about how to pray and seek answers from God. Does it mean that you should not also seek wise counsel when you face a major decision? No, for it is always prudent to seek wise counsel concerning major decisions. However, no matter what any counselor may advise, the final decision and the responsibility for it always belong to you.

DISTINGUISHING OF SPIRITS

This gift provides a very specialized kind of knowledge—the identification of the spirit or spirits controlling a situation. This knowledge comes directly from the Holy Spirit to the recipient, letting him know whether it is the Holy Spirit, mere human motivation, or demonic power operating in the situation. In cases where demonic powers are operating, the Holy Spirit will also often reveal the identities of the key spirits at work, through a word of knowledge. John wrote:

> Beloved, do not believe every spirit, but test the spirits to see whether they are from God, because many false prophets have gone out into the world. By this you know the Spirit of God: every spirit that confesses that Jesus Christ has come in the flesh is from God; and every spirit that does not confess Jesus is not from God; this is the spirit of the antichrist, of which you have heard that it is coming, and now it is already in the world. [1 John 4:1–3]

There are natural human fears, but there are also various kinds of demonic spirits of fear. There are natural human attitudes of meanness, bigotry, and hatred, but there are also demonic spirits of hatred, violence, and murder. This gift is especially valuable when you are actively engaged in spiritual warfare.

15–3

VOCAL GIFTS — VARIOUS KINDS OF TONGUES

Vocal gifts are most often given through the Holy Spirit in one of two settings: when we are by ourselves, and when we are in a church service. The gifts are the same regardless of the setting. The ways these gifts are expressed in a church service are subject to the directions and restrictions in 1 Corinthians 14. Those restrictions do not apply to one's private prayer time.

A person speaking in tongues is speaking words that are being provided by the Holy Spirit. They are speaking in a true language, but it is not a language that the speaker has learned or understands. The first biblical account of someone speaking in tongues occurred on the Day of Pentecost, "And they were all filled with the Holy Spirit and began to speak with other tongues, as the Spirit was giving them utterance" (Acts 2:4).

Many of those people were speaking in known languages which they had never learned, as Acts 2:5–12 describes. Churches that encourage this spiritual gift among their members and in their church services are described as Pentecostal (named after the Day of Pentecost) or Charismatic (after the Greek word *charis*, meaning "gift").*

I still remember very clearly the first time I heard anyone speak in tongues, even though it happened almost forty years ago. In September of 1969 Brenda and I moved from Atlanta, Georgia, to Orlando, Florida, because I had accepted a job there. In early December of that year I flew back to Atlanta and successfully defended my doctoral thesis to my thesis committee. On Sunday morning I attended Mount Paran Church of God. In those days, the pastor set aside time during the service when the people could pray privately about personal needs and concerns. I poured my heart out to the Lord that morning, first thanking Him for helping me complete my doctoral degree but then expressing my deep concern because we had not yet made any friends in Orlando nor had we found the right church. The uncertainty of the future, while trivial in retrospect, almost overwhelmed me as I prayed. I ended my prayer with the admission, "Lord, I feel so afraid!"

I was sitting in the center section near the back of the church. As soon as I had finished my prayer, a woman near the front of the church on the right side stood up and began speaking in tongues. As I related earlier, I had read about this in John Sherrill's book *They Speak with Other Tongues*, but I had never before heard it. As part of my doctoral program at Georgia Tech, I had taken two years of a foreign language. While the woman was speaking, I was listening intently, trying to determine if what I was hearing had the structure and vocabulary of a real language, or if it just sounded like some sort of gibberish or baby talk. I decided that it sounded like a real language, although I had no idea what language it might be, or even if it was an existing earthly language.

When she finished speaking in tongues, she sat down and the pastor began to interpret. I did not listen closely to the first part, but his interpretation ended with the words, "Do not be afraid." Tears streamed down my face as I realized that God had not only heard my prayer, He had "interrupted" a

---

* Babylon Ltd., *Charis*.

church service of probably fourteen hundred worshipers to speak a word of encouragement to me. It was a word that I desperately needed to hear from Him! Even now, almost forty years later, I still get tears whenever I share this with anyone, including right now as I am typing this paragraph. As a result of that experience, I have never doubted the reality, the validity, or the relevance of the spiritual gifts of various kinds of tongues and the interpretation of tongues.

PRIVATE PRAYER

As I said, there are two primary contexts in which people speak in tongues—in their private devotions and in a church service. Let's look at 1 Corinthians 14 and see how it applies to private prayers. The key verses are 2, 14, and 15, "For one who speaks in a tongue does not speak to men but to God; for no one understands, but in his spirit he speaks mysteries" (2).

People speaking in tongues to God in prayer do not normally understand what they are praying. They are praying from their spirit, not from their understanding, as Paul explained a few verses later:

> For if I pray in a tongue, my spirit prays, but my mind is unfruitful. What is the outcome then? I will pray with the spirit and I will pray with the mind also; I will sing with the spirit and I shall sing with the mind also. [1 Corinthians 14:14–15]

Praying with the spirit is praying in tongues. Singing with the spirit is singing in tongues. The singing can be either to the melody of a known song, or to an impromptu melody that the Holy Spirit gives you in the same way that He gives you the words you sing.

An important reason for praying in tongues, or praying with the spirit, is for personal edification. To *edify* means "to uplift, to enlighten, to instruct, to guide, to inform, and to prepare."* We are personally benefited in one or more of these ways whenever we pray in tongues. I don't know about you, but for me there is never a time when I would not like to be benefited in those ways.

If you desire that the Lord use you to bring spiritual gifts to others, this is the place to begin because praying in tongues involves only you and the Holy Spirit in privacy. There is no one else to hear you. There is no one else

---

* Merriam Webster Inc., *Edify*.

before whom you might feel inhibited or intimidated or embarrassed. There are only you and the Holy Spirit. If you are unwilling to exercise this gift privately, you cannot expect the Holy Spirit to use you in a public setting for this or any of the other spiritual gifts.

An easy way to get started is to select a need that you have, or a need that someone else has, ask the Holy Spirit to help you pray, and then just start praying. Paul described this in Romans 8:

> In the same way the Spirit also helps our weakness; for we do not know how to pray as we should, but the Spirit Himself intercedes for us with groanings too deep for words; and He who searches the hearts knows what the mind of the Spirit is, because He intercedes for the saints according to the will of God. [26–27]

PUBLIC MINISTRY

When a person speaks aloud in tongues in a church service and someone interprets, there are many people present who may potentially be edified. 1 Corinthians 14 addresses edifying the church in verses 4, 5, 12, and 26 as do Romans 14:19, 15:2, and Ephesians 4:29. So whenever you feel led to speak in tongues in church, keep in mind that it is God's purpose to edify His people through this gift.

Unlike the knowledge gifts, where we may sometimes not realize that we have been given one, we will be keenly aware whenever we are used to bring one of the vocal spiritual gifts in church. The usual setting in which the Holy Spirit prompts someone to speak forth in tongues is a mixed gathering of Christians and others. If you are the one to speak forth, you will usually feel both an anointing and a prompting to speak. Feeling an anointing is not enough, for the anointing you feel could be an anointing for you to pray, or to lay hands on someone, or it could be just that you feel the presence of the Holy Spirit. When you feel both an anointing and a prompting to speak, wait for the proper timing, the right opportunity. Speaking forth at the wrong time, rather than being a blessing, can be an interruption in the flow of what the Holy Spirit is doing in the service.

Bringing a vocal spiritual gift in a way that edifies the church and speaks to the intended individual or individuals is always initiated and orchestrated by the Holy Spirit. It also requires cooperation among the person who is to speak, the pastor, and whoever is leading the service at the moment (for instance, the song leader). It requires each of them to be sensitive to the leading of the Holy Spirit. The person who speaks in tongues should stand and speak distinctly and loudly enough to be easily heard by all in attendance. Then the person to whom the Holy Spirit has given the interpretation should stand promptly and speak loudly and clearly enough that all can hear and be edified. The pastor and the person leading the service must remain sensitive to the leading of the Holy Spirit and pause to permit God to speak to His people.

Sometimes the right opportunity to bring a vocal spiritual gift never occurs. I have been in many Pentecostal and Charismatic services where the pastor and the song leader never allowed enough of a pause in the service for the Holy Spirit "to get a word in edgewise." One reason may be that the pastor and the song leader were so involved in presenting their own program that they had become insensitive to the leading of the Holy Spirit. Another could be that the church leadership had made a conscious decision to discourage or even to disallow vocal spiritual gifts in the church services. Such a decision directly contradicts Scripture, "Do not quench the Spirit; do not despise prophetic utterances" (1 Thessalonians 5:19–20).

On the other hand, I have been in numerous services where the pastor was sensitive to the leading of the Holy Spirit, pausing at just the right time during the singing, the prayer time, or even during the sermon, to allow the Holy Spirit to speak through the gifts of tongues and interpretation, or prophecy. It is a delight and a privilege, and it is very edifying, to be in such church services.

Although it is not the norm, over the years I have heard people relate incidents in which someone, speaking in tongues in a language that they did not know, was actually speaking a direct message to someone who was present, in that person's native language. Hearing such a direct word from God often has even more of an impact on someone than when God first spoke to me through tongues and interpretation. Do not quench the Holy Spirit (1 Thessalonians 5:19), for in doing so you may be directly interfering with what God wants to do for someone in the church service.

Suppose you feel an anointing and a prompting to speak forth in tongues. How can you really be sure that this is what you are supposed to do? The answer is that you will almost never be 100% certain. This is simply another example of walking by faith. Wait for what seems to be the right opportunity, speak forth clearly and boldly, and trust God that you are doing the right thing. At the same time, trust Him that when you do make a mistake, you may be embarrassed, but no real harm will be done.

There is one more thing. The Bible says that tongues in church should be interpreted. If you do not know that there is someone present whom the Lord regularly uses to interpret tongues, you must either be prepared for the Holy Spirit to use you to bring the interpretation, or you are obliged not to speak forth in tongues (1 Corinthians 14:13, 27–28).

15–4

VOCAL GIFTS — THE INTERPRETATION OF TONGUES

Paul, addressing speaking in tongues in church, wrote:

> There are, perhaps, a great many kinds of languages in the world, and no kind is without meaning. If then I do not know the meaning of the language, I will be to the one who speaks a barbarian, and the one who speaks will be a barbarian to me... Therefore let one who speaks in a tongue pray that he may interpret. [1 Corinthians 14:10–11, 13]

The interpretation of tongues is a companion gift to the gift of various kinds of tongues. God uses them together to edify the hearers. Without someone's giving the interpretation, most people in the church service will not know what God's message was. I said that most would not know, rather than that no one would know, for two reasons. First, if the tongues are spoken in a language known to some of the hearers, then they will know what was said. Second, it is not unusual for several of the believers to be given the interpretation simultaneously, so that all of them know the essence of what was said. It then behooves one of them to speak forth the interpretation, so that everyone else may also know what was said and thereby be edified.

After the interpretation has been given, if the pastor or person leading the meeting believes it to be from God, he should so indicate by an appropriate response. If he believes it is not valid, he should continue to pause, perhaps saying something like, "Does someone else have an interpretation?"

An interpretation is not necessarily a translation. It is typically either a reiteration or a synopsis of the message, spoken in the style and vocabulary of the person interpreting. That is one reason why an interpretation may be noticeably longer or shorter than the tongues. Also, although God uses proper grammar, the interpreter may not. Grammatical errors do not invalidate an interpretation.

I remember being in a church service when a message in tongues was spoken, and I believed that I had the interpretation. I stood and spoke in my own style, which tends to be succinct and to the point. Although the pastor knew who I was, this was the first time that the Lord had used me for interpretation in that particular church. It was immediately obvious that the pastor did not accept my interpretation. I thought, "Oh, well, maybe I missed it." After a short pause, the pastor's mother-in-law, an elderly and very godly woman, rose and gave an interpretation. She spoke much more fluently and eloquently than I, but the essence of her interpretation was the same as mine. I felt both relieved and vindicated. Do not be afraid to step out in bringing tongues or an interpretation. Allow the Holy Spirit to use you in those gifts.

15–5

VOCAL GIFTS — PROPHECY

The Apostle Peter described prophecies in the Old Testament in this way, "…for no prophecy was ever made by an act of human will, but men moved by the Holy Spirit spoke from God" (2 Peter 1:21).

The vocal spiritual gift of prophecy has this in common with prophecy in Scripture: men and women moved by the Holy Spirit speak forth a specific message from God for a specific audience. The primary difference is that prophecies in the Bible have been judged and validated through thousands of years. "Fresh" prophecies are subjected to much less stringent judging and validation, "Let two or three prophets speak, and let the others pass judgment" (1 Corinthians 14:29).

Fresh prophecies, even though validated by other contemporary prophets, can never carry the weight of authenticity of prophecies in the Bible. The primary standard for judging fresh prophecies is their degree of alignment with what the Bible teaches. Because the Holy Spirit is the author of the Bible, and He is the one who provides genuine prophecies, both the prophecy and the Bible will be in perfect agreement when the prophecy is genuine.

The message of most prophecies is for one or more of the following purposes:

- Edification, "…one who prophesies edifies the church" (1 Corinthians 14:4b); and "Let all things be done for edification" (26c).
- Exhortation, "For you can all prophesy one by one, so that all may learn and all may be exhorted;" (31).
- Consolation, "But one who prophesies speaks to men for edification and exhortation and consolation" (3).
- Revelation, "But if a revelation is made to another who is seated, the first one must keep silent" (30).

Prophecies that are warnings are not precluded nor are predictive prophecies, but those occur much less frequently and should be subjected to more rigorous judging before they are accepted as valid.

In the same way that the Holy Spirit will anoint you and prompt you to speak forth in tongues or to interpret tongues, He will anoint you and prompt you to speak forth in prophecy. Sometimes He will give you the prophecy hours, days, or even further ahead of time, rehearsing it with you over and over until you can deliver it correctly. At other times, you will know that you are to speak a word of prophecy, but you will not know its content until you stand to speak. For the seemingly impromptu urgings, probably your most important responsibility is to cease speaking when the Holy Spirit ceases speaking. It is not uncommon for a novice to speak forth a true word of prophecy. Then, when he should have stopped and sat down, he continues by expounding on one of his favorite doctrines or themes. When that happens, an experienced pastor will usually indulge him for a short time before saying something like, "Thank you, brother," and then proceeding with the service. As with tongues and interpretation, the pastor should indicate to the congregation his concurrence with the word spoken when he believes it is a true word from God.

Sometimes the message from the Holy Spirit through tongues and interpretation or prophecy will contain an encouragement to pray or to "seek My face." Sometimes it will contain an encouragement to action such as, "I delight in your praise." The pastor should respond to the Holy Spirit, turn aside from the agenda, and lead the congregation in doing as God has said. God speaks for a purpose. Blessings occur when we heed His word and follow Him.

15–6

POWER GIFTS

The three power gifts are faith, gifts of healing, and effecting of miracles. We will look at all three of these in this chapter.

FAITH

Faith is related to believing, but they are not the same thing. A belief is a conviction, an intuition, a conclusion, or a persuasion that something is true. Beliefs are usually arrived at through a thought process. Believing is, in many cases, a predecessor and a precondition of faith.

Faith is an assurance, a confidence, or a certainty that something is true. Believing can become more convinced and more persuaded over time. But believing, no matter how hard or for how long, does not transform itself into faith. That fact has frustrated untold numbers of sincere Christians who have "believed" for a healing, for a miracle, or for a loved one to be saved and have subsequently been disappointed.

Faith comes from God. It is imparted by Him. Each gift of faith is a one-time impartation of faith through the Holy Spirit for a specific purpose. Our part in receiving a gift of faith is to become attuned to the Father, to Jesus, and to the Holy Spirit.

The purpose of a gift of faith is to enable us to victoriously overcome or to patiently endure trials, obstacles, and calamities because we can see the eternal reward (read Hebrews 11). A gift of faith provides us with an eternal perspective—God's perspective—about a situation.

One other thought about gifts of faith. Healing is not a proper subject of a gift of faith. Healing is the subject of gifts of healing. Likewise, a miracle is not a proper subject of a gift of faith. A miracle is the subject of effecting of miracles.

GIFTS OF HEALING

God has available to Him a wide variety of mechanisms through which He can heal us. There are the healing capabilities that He designed into our bodies, assisted by doctors, surgeons, nurses, hospitals, and medications. There is the laying on of hands by believers, "These signs will accompany those who have believed…they will lay hands on the sick, and they will recover "(Mark 16:17a, 18c).

There is prayer and anointing with oil by the elders of the church:

> Is anyone among you sick? Then he must call for the elders of the church and they are to pray over him, anointing him with oil in the name of the Lord; and the prayer offered in faith will restore the one who is sick, and the Lord will raise him up, and if he has committed sins, they will be forgiven him. [James 5:14–15]

There are prayers by believers for one another:

> Therefore, confess your sins to one another, and pray for one another so that you may be healed. The effective prayer of a righteous man can accomplish much. [James 5:16]

Jesus gave believers authority over demons. Thus sicknesses that are caused by demonic power are subject to being healed through a believer exercising his spiritual authority in Jesus' name, "And He called the twelve together, and gave them power and authority over all the demons and to heal diseases" (Luke 9:1).

In each of these ways, a person initiates a request for God's healing, either on behalf of himself or herself, or on behalf of another. God can also sovereignly initiate healing through one of the gifts of the Spirit: gifts of healing. My Interlinear Greek New Testament translates "gifts of healings" as "gifts of cures." I like that wording because it helps clarify for me the boundary between things that fall within the category of healings and things that fall within the category of miracles. Healings cover conditions, sicknesses, diseases, and wounds—things that either would not occur in a healthy body or that a healthy body could eventually recover from. Miracles cover the rest, including instantaneous healings, restoring lost faculties (e.g., hearing, eyesight), restoring ill-formed or missing body parts, raising the dead, as well as anything else that requires suspending or superseding the normal laws of nature.

The gifts of healing are most readily apparent in healing revivals, evangelistic meetings where the Lord authenticates the gospel message through performing signs and wonders. This is in accordance with the prayer of the early church in Acts 4:

"And now, Lord,... grant that Your bond-servants may speak Your word with all confidence, while You extend Your hand to heal, and signs and wonders take place through the name of Your holy servant Jesus." [Acts 4:29–30]

When you need to be the recipient of a gift of healing, my recommendation is to find a church or a ministry through whom God is known to administer gifts of healing. But don't lose sight of the fact that the source of all healing is God Himself, not the person through whom He delivers it, "For I, the Lord, am your healer" (Exodus 15:26c).

EFFECTING OF MIRACLES

The Greek word translated as *miracles* is *dunamis*, and it means "power, might, or strength." *Dunamis* is derived from the Greek word *dunamai*, which means "to be able, to have power."* In the New American Standard Bible, *dunamis* is translated "miracle," "miracles," or "miraculous powers" approximately twenty times. It is translated "power" or "powers" approximately ninety times.

Every miracle is a demonstration of God's power. The normal purpose of a miracle is the same as that of a gift of healing: to authenticate the preached word, "God also testifying with them, both by signs and wonders and by various miracles and gifts of the Holy Spirit according to His own will" (Hebrews 2:4).

Miracles are more dramatic than healings. While healings usually occur gradually over some period of time, miracles are often instantaneous. While healings mainly address sicknesses, diseases, and wounds, miracles can restore hearing, sight, and dysfunctional organs and limbs. Miracles can even restore or create missing body parts, or raise the dead.

God was performing extraordinary miracles by the hands of Paul, so that handkerchiefs or aprons were even carried from his body to the sick, and the diseases left them and the evil spirits went out. [Acts 19:11–12]

As with gifts of healing, if you need a miracle for yourself, my recommendation is to find a church or a ministry through whom God is known to distribute gifts of miracles.

* Babylon Ltd., *Dunamis*.

15–7

THE SPECIAL SIGNIFICANCE OF HEALINGS AND MIRACLES

As I wrote earlier, signs and wonders, including healings and miracles, have special significance in convincing people of the authenticity of the message being preached. Jesus used healings and miracles to authenticate His message and to demonstrate that He was who He said He was. Let's explore this idea further by reading some incidents from Jesus' ministry.

The first incident happened at the wedding in Cana of Galilee. John 1 says that two days before, John and Andrew had heard Jesus speak and concluded that He was the Messiah. They told Simon and then took him to meet Jesus. Because this miracle is reported only in John's gospel, some have suggested that this may have been John's own wedding.

> On the third day there was a wedding in Cana of Galilee, and the mother of Jesus was there; and both Jesus and His disciples were invited to the wedding. When the wine ran out, the mother of Jesus said to Him, "They have no wine." And Jesus said to her, "Woman, what does that have to do with us? My hour has not yet come." His mother said to the servants, "Whatever He says to you, do it." Now there were six stone waterpots set there for the Jewish custom of purification, containing twenty or thirty gallons each. Jesus said to them, "Fill the waterpots with water." So they filled them up to the brim. And He said to them, "Draw some out now and take it to the headwaiter." So they took it to him. When the headwaiter tasted the water which had become wine, and did not know where it came from (but the servants who had drawn the water knew), the headwaiter called the bridegroom, and said to him, "Every man serves the good wine first, and when the people have drunk freely, then he serves the poorer wine; but you have kept the good wine until now." **This beginning of His signs Jesus did in Cana of Galilee, and manifested His glory, and His disciples believed in Him.** [John 2:1–11]

When Jesus turned water into wine, it was a kindness to the bridegroom. But it served a larger purpose: it helped His disciples believe in Him!

The next incident occurred soon afterwards:

Now it happened that while the crowd was pressing around Him and listening to the word of God, He was standing by the lake of Gennesaret; and He saw two boats lying at the edge of the lake; but the fishermen had gotten out of them and were washing their nets. And He got into one of the boats, which was Simon's, and asked him to put out a little way from the land. And He sat down and began teaching the people from the boat. When He had finished speaking, He said to Simon, "Put out into the deep water and let down your nets for a catch." Simon answered and said, "Master, we worked hard all night and caught nothing, but I will do as You say and let down the nets." When they had done this, they enclosed a great quantity of fish, and their nets began to break; so they signaled to their partners in the other boat for them to come and help them. And they came and filled both of the boats, so that they began to sink. **But when Simon Peter saw that**, he fell down at Jesus' feet, saying, "Go away from me Lord, for I am a sinful man, O Lord!" For **amazement had seized him and all his companions because of the catch of fish which they had taken; and so also were James and John, sons of Zebedee, who were partners with Simon**. And Jesus said to Simon, "Do not fear, from now on you will be catching men." When they had brought their boats to land, they left everything and followed Him. [Luke 5:1–11]

Before Jesus called Peter, James, and John to be His disciples, He performed a miracle to demonstrate who He was. That miracle—a net-breaking, boat-sinking catch of fish—was tailored to His audience of professional fishermen. The result was that they left everything and followed Him.

John the Baptist, some time after baptizing Jesus in the Jordan River and seeing the Holy Spirit descend upon Him, was arrested and imprisoned. In his prison cell, he heard about Jesus' ministry. But John began to question in his own mind whether Jesus was indeed the promised Messiah:

Summoning two of his disciples, John sent them to the Lord, saying, "Are You the Expected One, or do we look for someone else?" When the men had come to Him, they said, "John the Baptist has sent us to You, to ask, 'Are You the Expected One, or do we look for someone else?'" At that very time He cured many people of diseases and afflictions and evil spirits; and He gave sight to many who were blind. And He answered and said to them, "Go and report to John what you have seen and heard: the blind receive sight, the lame walk, the lepers are cleansed, and the deaf hear, the dead are raised up, the poor have the gospel preached to them. Blessed is he who does not take offense at Me." [Luke 7:19–23]

Jesus did not just verbally answer John the Baptist's question. First He demonstrated who He was through healings and miracles. Then He told John's disciples to report back everything that they had seen and heard.

On three separate occasions, Jesus said that we should believe in Him because of the works that He performed, "But the testimony which I have is greater than the testimony of John; for the works which the Father has given me to accomplish—**the very works that I do—testify about Me,** that the Father has sent Me" (John 5:36); "If I do not do the works of My Father, do not believe Me; but if I do them, though you do not believe Me, **believe the works,** so that you may know and understand that the Father is in Me, and I in the Father" (John 10:37–38); "Believe Me that I am in the Father and the Father is in Me; otherwise **believe because of the works** themselves" (John 14:11).

Notice what Peter said about Jesus on the Day of Pentecost, and then at Cornelius' house:

> "Men of Israel, listen to these words: Jesus the Nazarene, a man **attested to you by God with miracles and wonders and signs which God performed through Him** in your midst, just as you yourselves know…You know of Jesus of Nazareth, how God anointed Him with the Holy Spirit and with power, and how He went about doing good and **healing all** who were oppressed by the devil, **for God was with Him."** [Acts 2:22; 10:38]

The healings and the miracles that God performed through Jesus were expressions of His love and compassion to their recipients. But their larger purpose was to authenticate Jesus' message and demonstrate that He was who He said He was.

Using signs and wonders to authenticate the message being preached did not end when Jesus ascended into heaven. The Book of Acts describes the healing of the lame man at the gate of the temple (3:1–3:11). It provided an opportunity for Peter to preach to the bystanders who witnessed the miracle or its results (3:12–3:26). Because of that, Peter and John were arrested (4:1–4:3), "But **many of those who had heard the message believed;** and the number of men came to be about five thousand" (Acts 4:4).

The next day, Peter and John witnessed about Jesus to an assembly that consisted of the high priest, others of high priestly descent, rulers, elders, and scribes. Those opportunities arose because of one miracle that God performed through them!

Consider what Philip the evangelist did in Samaria, "The crowds with one accord were giving attention to what was said by Philip, as they heard and saw the signs which he was performing" (Acts 8:6).

Consider Peter's miracle of healing in the city of Lydda:

> There he found a man named Aeneas, who had been bedridden eight years, for he was paralyzed. Peter said to him, "Aeneas, Jesus Christ heals you; get up, and make your bed." Immediately he got up. **And all who lived at Lydda and Sharon saw him, and they turned to the Lord.** [Acts 9:33–35]

Consider signs and wonders done by Paul in the city of Iconium.

> Therefore they spent a long time there speaking boldly with reliance upon the Lord, who was testifying to the word of His grace, granting that signs and wonders be done by their hands. [Acts 14:3]

Those examples amply illustrate what Mark wrote:

> And they went out and preached everywhere, while the Lord worked with them, and confirmed the word by the signs that followed. [Mark 16:20]

Later, the writer of Hebrews wrote:

> For if the word spoken through angels proved unalterable, and every transgression and disobedience received a just penalty, how will we escape if we neglect so great a salvation? After it was at the first spoken through the Lord, it was confirmed to us by those who heard, **God also testifying with them, both by signs and wonders and by various miracles and by gifts of the Holy Spirit according to His own will.** [2:2–4]

And Paul wrote, "…for our gospel did not come to you in word only, but also in power and in the Holy Spirit and with full conviction…" (1 Thessalonians 1:5a).

I see two extremes in the modern church. On the one hand, many churches deny the validity of spiritual gifts, some actively prohibiting them. This leads to a greatly weakened church. On the other hand, other churches create such an extreme atmosphere of "encouraging" spiritual gifts that it discredits both those churches and the genuine gifts of the Holy Spirit. Let us reaffirm the need for God to perform healings and miracles today, by the power of the Holy Spirit, to authenticate the preached message about Jesus:

> And now, Lord, take note of their threats, and grant that Your bond-servants may speak Your word with all confidence, while You extend You hand to heal, and signs and wonders take place through the name of Your holy servant Jesus. [Acts 4:29–30]

SPIRIT-EMPOWERED MINISTRIES

16–1

SPIRIT-EMPOWERED MINISTRIES IN THE CHURCH

When Paul introduced spiritual gifts in the first part of 1 Corinthians 12, he also introduced Spirit-empowered ministries, "And there are varieties of ministries, and the same Lord" (1 Corinthians 12:5).

Near the end of that chapter, he enumerated some of those ministries:

> And God has appointed in the church, first apostles, second prophets, third teachers, then miracles, then gifts of healings, helps, administrations, various kinds of tongues. [28]

In his letter to the church in Ephesus, Paul wrote this about Jesus and Spirit-empowered ministries:

> "When He ascended on high…He gave gifts to me."…And He gave some as apostles, and some as prophets, and some as evangelists, and some as pastors and teachers, for the equipping of the saints for the work of service, to the building up of the body of Christ; [Ephesians 4:8a, 8c, 11–12]

Thus ministers and ministries are gifts from Jesus to His church. Jesus intends that Spirit-empowered ministers and ministries function within the context of the church and be integral parts of it, "But now God has placed the members, each one of them, in the body, just as He desired." (1 Corinthians 12:18).

UNITY IN VARIETY

1 Corinthians 12 compares Jesus' spiritual body, the church, to the human body that He has given us. Like the human body, the church:

- Contains a wide variety of diverse parts.
- Performs a wide variety of diverse functions.
- Is a single cohesive organism.

The book of 1 Peter makes a similar point but uses the metaphor of a building rather than the metaphor of the human body. Peter wrote:

> And coming to Him as to a living stone which has been rejected by men, but is choice and precious in the sight of God, you also, as living stones, are being built up as a spiritual house for a holy priesthood, to offer up spiritual sacrifices acceptable to God through Jesus Christ. [1 Peter 2:4–5]

It is important to notice that those verses in 1 Peter use the analogy of stones, rather than bricks, as the primary building material. Stones are unique items. Each is recognizable as being a stone, yet no two stones are identical. Stones come in a wide variety of materials, colors, sizes, and shapes. They become smoother and more rounded, losing the sharpness of their edges, as they rub against other stones.

God did not intend to build a church from identical bricks, and we err whenever we try to do so. Bricks are uniform in size, shape, color, and strength. They are much easier than stones to build with because they are interchangeable. God is not looking for uniformity. He desires uniqueness in each component of His church. God builds with stones, not with bricks. As simple as that concept seems, it is difficult to grasp and implement. Otherwise, the Holy Spirit would have led Paul to write 1 Corinthians 12 differently. Let's look at this passage from the perspective of God's desire for variety and uniqueness.

Notice these phrases from verses 4, 5, and 6:

> …**varieties** of gifts, but the same Spirit.
> …**varieties** of ministries, and the same Lord.
> …**varieties** of effects, but the same God.

Having varieties of gifts, ministries, and effects was God's idea! Now notice verse 7, "But to each one is given the manifestation of the Spirit for the common good."

There are varieties of gifts because there are varieties of human needs. There are varieties of ministries to share the workload, to allow multiple people to minister, and to match ministries to the personalities and capabilities of individuals. When each type of ministry is functioning and the ministry load is being properly shared, the church is greatly benefited.

One of the Holy Spirit's objectives is to make His spiritual gifts widely available. He does not intend that they be distributed through only a few select individuals. That is clear from verses 8 to 10:

> For **to one** is given…and **to another**…**to another**…and **to another** …and **to another**…and **to another**…and **to another**…and **to another**…and **to another**…

Then verse 11 says, "But one and the same Spirit works all these things, distributing to each one individually just as **He wills.**"

It is not our choice which gift or gifts He delivers through us. Our function is to humbly and willingly allow ourselves to be used by the Holy Spirit, being faithful to deliver spiritual gifts from Him to their intended recipients.

Continuing in 1 Corinthians 12, we see that Christ is not divided. He does not have, for instance, a Roman Catholic body, a mainstream Protestant body, an evangelical body, a Pentecostal body, and an independent body. There is only *one* body of Christ and everyone who confesses Jesus as his Savior is a member of His body. That is true regardless of our denominational affiliation or lack thereof. It is true regardless of the other beliefs that we may have. We Christians are all parts of one body, whether or not we have yet recognized it or acknowledged it:

> For even as the body is one and yet has many members, and all the members of the body, though they are many, are one body, so also is Christ. For by one Spirit we were all baptized into one body, whether Jews or Greeks, whether slaves or free, and we were all made to drink of one Spirit. For the body is not one member, but many. [1 Corinthians 12:12–14]

FEELINGS OF INFERIORITY

Though we are all members of one body, our roles are not all the same. As a result, some parts of the body—some ministers and some members—may feel inferior, unneeded, or left out because their role does not seem important enough.

> If the foot says, "Because I am not a hand, I am not a part of the body," it is not for this reason any less a part of the body. And if the ear says,

> "Because I am not an eye, I am not a part of the body," it is not for this reason any less a part of the body. [1 Corinthians 12:15–16]

Paul assures us that every minister and every member is needed and has a valuable function to perform.

> If the whole body were an eye, where would the hearing be? If the whole were hearing, where would the sense of smell be? But now God has placed the members, each one of them, in the body, just as He desired. If they were all one member, where would the body be? [1 Corinthians 12:17–19]

> For just as we have many members in one body and all the members do not have the same function, so we, who are many, are one body in Christ, and individually members one of another. [Romans 12:4–5]

Rejoice with me that we are stones—unique and valuable members of Christ's body—each with our own individualized roles to perform. God intends it to be that way. Let us discover our roles and function joyfully, enthusiastically, and faithfully in them.

FEELINGS OF SUPERIORITY

After addressing feelings of inferiority on the part of some ministers and members of the body, Paul cautions others against having an attitude of superiority or exclusivity. We are all necessary and we are all, in that sense, equal members of the body.

> But now there are many members, but one body. And the eye cannot say to the hand, "I have no need of you"; or again the head to the feet, "I have no need of you." On the contrary, it is much truer that the members of the body which seem to be weaker are necessary; and those members of the body, which we deem less honorable, on these we bestow more abundant honor, and our less presentable members become much more presentable, whereas our more presentable members have no need of it. But God has so composed the body, giving more abundant honor to that member which lacked, so that there may be no division in the body, but that the members may have the same care for one another. [1 Corinthians 12:20–25]

The next verse tells us that we should treat one another without rivalry or jealousy, but with love, honor, and compassion as fellow members of Christ's body, "And if one member suffers, all the members suffer with it; if one member is honored, all the members rejoice with it" (1 Corinthians 12:26).

The human body, which Paul used as an analogy for the church throughout 1 Corinthians 12, is not amorphous. It has intricate structure and order. In the same way, it is God's intention that Christ's body, the church worldwide, has structure and order. To achieve that, He established ministries and placed them in the church in proper relationship to one another.

16–2

SPIRIT-EMPOWERED MINISTRIES DESCRIBED

Five ministries are identified in Ephesians 4:11:

- Apostle
- Prophet
- Evangelist
- Pastor
- Teacher

Let us look together at the primary functions of each ministry and the spiritual gifts that are most important for a person to be effective in that ministry. Apart from the gifts of the Holy Spirit, no ministry can achieve the effectiveness that God intends and the needs demand. And in the same way that no two people are identical, we cannot expect any two ministers or any two ministries to be exactly alike.

APOSTLE

Jesus was the first apostle, established by the Father as an example for us, "Therefore, holy brethren, partakers of a heavenly calling, consider Jesus, the Apostle and High Priest of our confession" (Hebrews 3:1).

Apostles take the gospel to new areas and establish churches there. For example, Paul was an apostle to the Gentiles, "To me, the very least of all saints, this grace was given, to preach to the Gentiles the unfathomable riches of Christ" (Ephesians 3:8).

An apostle needs every spiritual gift, especially the gifts of faith, healing, and effecting of miracles, "The signs of a true apostle were performed among you with all perseverance, by signs and wonders and miracles" (2 Corinthians 12:12).

Some in the church today do not consider being an apostle a valid ministry. But Paul is very clear about its validity:

> And He [Jesus] gave some as apostles, and some as prophets, and some as evangelists, and some as pastors and teachers, for the equipping of the saints for the work of service, to the building up of the body of Christ; **until** we all attain to the unity of the faith, and the knowledge of the Son of God, to a mature man, to the measure of stature which belongs to the fullness of Christ. [Ephesians 4:11-13]

The church as a whole has not yet fulfilled the conditions of the "until" clause. Therefore the ministries of apostles, prophets, evangelists, pastors, and teachers are still very much needed "for the equipping of the saints for the work of service."

PROPHET

Prophets speak direct messages from God. The gift of prophecy is essential to functioning in this ministry:

> Now at this time some prophets came down from Jerusalem to Antioch. One of them named Agabus stood up and began to indicate by the Spirit that there would certainly be a great famine all over the world. And this took place in the reign of Claudius...And Judas and Silas, also being prophets themselves, encouraged and strengthened the brethren with a lengthy message. [Acts 11:27–28; 15:32]

EVANGELIST

An evangelist proclaims the gospel of salvation to unbelievers. The gifts of prophecy, a word of knowledge, a word of wisdom, and distinguishing of spirits are important to knowing the right message to preach. The gifts of faith, healing, and effecting of miracles are important to authenticate the message being preached:

> Philip went down to the city of Samaria and began proclaiming Christ to them. The crowds with one accord were giving attention to what was said by Philip, as they heard and saw the signs which he was performing. For in the case of many who had unclean spirits, they were coming out of them shouting with a loud voice; and many who had been paralyzed and lame were healed. [Acts 8:5–7]

PASTOR

Pastors oversee and care for people within a local church. The gifts of interpretation of tongues, prophecy, faith, a word of knowledge, a word of wisdom, and distinguishing of spirits are all important to ministering effectively as a pastor:

> Therefore, I exhort the elders among you, as your fellow elder and witness of the sufferings of Christ, and a partaker also of the glory that is to be revealed, shepherd the flock of God among you, exercising oversight not under compulsion, but voluntarily, according to the will of God; and not for sordid gain, but with eagerness; nor yet as lording it over those allotted to your charge, but proving to be examples to the flock. [1 Peter 5:1–3]

TEACHER

Teachers topically organize and present biblical truth and ways to apply it. A word of knowledge and a word of wisdom greatly enhance the effectiveness of teachers, "But as for you, speak the things which are fitting for sound doctrine" (Titus 2:1).

First Corinthians 12:28 lists five additional ministries:

- Effecting of miracles
- Gifts of healing
- Helps
- Administrations
- Various kinds of tongues

EFFECTING OF MIRACLES

A person with this ministry is regularly used by the Holy Spirit for the effecting of miracles. A word of knowledge, a word of wisdom, and distinguishing of spirits are also very valuable to ministering effectively, "And Stephen, full of grace and power, was performing great wonders and signs among the people" (Acts 6:8).

> God was performing extraordinary miracles by the hands of Paul, so that handkerchiefs or aprons were even carried from his body to the sick and the diseases left them and the evil spirits went out. [Acts 19:11-12]

GIFTS OF HEALING

Someone with this ministry is regularly used by the Holy Spirit to minister gifts of healing. In the functioning of this gift, a word of knowledge, a word of wisdom, and distinguishing of spirits are very valuable, "...and many who had been paralyzed and lame were healed" (Acts 8:7b).

> After this had happened, the rest of the people on the island who had diseases were coming to him and getting cured. [Acts 28:9]

HELPS

The ministry of helps provides practical assistance, especially to other ministers. A word of wisdom, a word of knowledge, and distinguishing of spirits are the gifts most frequently needed in order to be effective in the ministry of helps, "And having sent into Macedonia two of those who ministered to him, Timothy and Erastus, he himself stayed in Asia for a while" (Acts 19:22).

> ...whom I wished to keep with me, so that on your behalf he [Onesimus] might minister to me in my imprisonment for the gospel. [Philemon 13]

ADMINISTRATIONS

Administrators organize and oversee supporting activities, including those involving finances. A word of wisdom, a word of knowledge, and distinguishing of spirits are the gifts most frequently needed in order to be effective.

…and not only this, but he has also been appointed by the churches to travel with us in this gracious work, which is being administered by us for the glory of the Lord Himself, and to show our readiness, taking precaution so that no one will discredit us in our administration of this generous gift. [2 Corinthians 8:19–20]

For the ministry of this service is not only fully supplying the needs of the saints, but is also overflowing through many thanksgivings to God. [2 Corinthians 9:12]

VARIOUS KINDS OF TONGUES

A person with this ministry is regularly used by the Holy Spirit to bring the gift of tongues publicly during church services. The gifts of various kinds of tongues and the interpretation of tongues are essential:

In the Law it is written, "By men of strange tongues and by the lips of strangers I will speak to this people, and even so they will not listen to Me," says the Lord. So then tongues are for a sign, not to those who believe but to unbelievers…If anyone speaks in a tongue, it should be by two or at the most three, and each in turn, and one must interpret; but if there is no interpreter, he must keep silent in the church; and let him speak to himself and to God. [1 Corinthians 14:21–22a; 27–28]

1 Corinthians 12:29–30 states the obvious: not every person has been given every ministry. Some people have one ministry and other people have another.

All are not apostles, are they? All are not prophets, are they? All are not teachers, are they? All are not workers of miracles, are they? All do not have gifts of healings, do they? All do not speak with tongues, do they? All do not interpret, do they?

Although the Holy Spirit can use any willing person to minister any spiritual gift, people primarily deliver those gifts that are needed in their ministry.

OTHER MINISTRIES

There are a multitude of ministries beyond those named in Ephesians 4:11 and 1 Corinthians 12:28. Romans 12:6–8 names some of them, but that list is not meant to be exhaustive. Whatever you do for other people is a ministry if you are called to it by Jesus and you actively depend upon the Holy Spirit to be effective in it. If you simply donate your time and apply your abilities and talents in response to a need, that is still a good thing, but it is more properly classified as "good works."

16–3

SPIRIT-EMPOWERED MINISTRIES— HOW WE ARE TO MINISTER

Let's see what the Bible says about the way we are to minister, especially the personal traits and attitudes that we are to display. The list is not lengthy, but it is important because our attitudes greatly impact our usefulness and effectiveness in ministering to others. Peter wrote, "As each one has received a special gift, employ it in serving one another, as good stewards of the manifold grace of God" (1 Peter 4:10).

Spirit-empowered ministries are Jesus' gifts to His church. Being entrusted with a Spirit-empowered ministry is God's grace to us. Our responsibility is to faithfully minister God's gifts and God's grace to those we serve.

Peter emphasized that ministers are to do their work with dedication and diligence, and by drawing their strength from God:

> Whoever speaks, is to do so as one who is speaking the utterances of God; whoever serves is to do so as one who is serving by the strength which God supplies; so that in all things God may be glorified through Jesus Christ, to whom belongs the glory and dominion forever and ever. Amen. [1 Peter 4:11]

Our objective must be to minister in such a way that God is glorified. Achieving this objective requires that we minister with integrity and effectiveness.

Paul wrote a similar exhortation:

> Since we have gifts that differ according to the grace given to us, each
> of us is to exercise them accordingly: if prophecy, according to the
> proportion of his faith; if service, in his serving; or he who teaches,
> in his teaching; or he who exhorts, in his exhortation; he who gives,
> with liberality; he who leads, with diligence; he who shows mercy, with
> cheerfulness. [Romans 12:6–8]

Look with me at 1 Corinthians 13, the well-known and often quoted
"Love Chapter." Notice its context. It follows 1 Corinthians 12, which introduces the gifts of the Holy Spirit, Spirit-empowered ministries, and the
concept that all ministries are necessary parts of the church. It precedes 1
Corinthians 14, which explains how to integrate the vocal gifts of the Holy
Spirit into the church service. As we read 1 Corinthians 13 together, notice
that the examples Paul uses all deal with ministering to others, and especially ministering gifts of the Holy Spirit. Notice also that Paul does not in
any way diminish the value of any of the gifts of the Holy Spirit to the person
who receives them. But he does illustrate the ways a minister can suffer crit-
icism and even discredit if he or she does not minister from a heart of love:

> If I speak with the tongues of men and of angels, but do not have love,
> I have become a noisy gong or a clanging cymbal. If I have the gift of
> prophecy, and know all mysteries and all knowledge; and if I have all
> faith, so as to remove mountains, but do not have love, I am nothing.
> And if I give all my possessions to feed the poor, and if I surrender
> my body to be burned, but do not have love, it profits me nothing. [1
> Corinthians 13:1–3]

Paul continues by describing what love looks like and how it behaves:

> Love is patient, love is kind and is not jealous; love does not brag and
> is not arrogant, does not act unbecomingly; it does not seek its own, is
> not provoked, does not take into account a wrong suffered, does not
> rejoice in unrighteousness, but rejoices with the truth; bears all things,
> believes all things, hopes all things, endures all things. Love never fails;
> [13:4–8a]

Then returning to the gifts of the Holy Spirit, Paul points out that they are temporal. Though they are needed now, they will no longer be needed after God's kingdom is fully manifested upon the earth. In contrast, love is an eternal quality; it will never cease to exist:

> ...but if there are gifts of prophecy, they will be done away; if there are tongues, they will cease; if there is knowledge, it will be done away. For we know in part and we prophesy in part; but when the perfect comes, the partial will be done away. When I was a child, I used to speak like a child, think like a child, reason like a child; when I became a man, I did away with childish things. For now we see in a mirror dimly, but then face to face; now I know in part, but then I will know fully just as I also have been fully known. But now faith, hope, love, abide these three; but the greatest of these is love. [1 Corinthians 13:8b-13]

Summing up the relationship between love and the gifts of the Holy Spirit, Paul says our goal is not *either* love *or* spiritual gifts; it is to manifest *both* love *and* spiritual gifts. We are to faithfully minister the gifts of the Holy Spirit, doing it with love, "Pursue love, yet desire earnestly spiritual gifts..." (1 Corinthians 14:1a).

In summary, Jesus gives spiritual ministries to individuals, and every Spirit-empowered ministry is needed in the church today. To function effectively in a Spirit-empowered ministry requires the availability of the appropriate spiritual gifts. It is the Holy Spirit who administers all spiritual gifts, distributing them as He wills. Apart from the Holy Spirit, no minister and no ministry can be fully effective. As we are led by Him, all things are possible. We are to minister to the needs of others in the same way that we want to be ministered to when we have needs: with integrity, with effectiveness, and with love. In the next several chapters we will address many of the ways the Holy Spirit works to develop those traits in us.

TRANSFORMED BY THE HOLY SPIRIT

17–1

TRANSFORMED BY
THE HOLY SPIRIT

Romans 12 describes the attitudes that we Christians should have, and how we should behave toward others. If we try, in our own strength, to conform to those qualities and behaviors, we can very quickly become discouraged. That is not what God desires. The key to understanding how to develop those qualities is found in the introductory verses of that chapter:

> Therefore I urge you, brethren, by the mercies of God, to present your bodies a living and holy sacrifice, acceptable to God, which is your spiritual service of worship. And do not be conformed to this world, but be transformed by the renewing of your mind, so that you may prove what the will of God is, that which is good and acceptable and perfect. [1–2]

The operative words in those verses are the command to "be transformed by the renewing of your mind." Our part in this process begins with deciding to obey this command and giving the Holy Spirit our permission to freely work on, in, and through us. Although we can learn to modify our behavior, the truth is that we are not able to transform ourselves. But the Holy Spirit can and will transform us as we cooperate with Him.

Galatians 5:19–21, which is written to Christians, describes how we often behave before we complete the process of transformation. We present a very unappealing portrait while we are still ruled by our fleshly desires:

> Now the deeds of the flesh are evident, which are: immorality, impurity, sensuality, idolatry, sorcery, enmities, strife, jealousy, outbursts of anger, disputes, dissensions, factions, envying, drunkenness, carousing, and things like these, of which I forewarn you, just as I have forewarned you, that those who practice such things will not inherit the kingdom of God.

1 Corinthians 6:9–11a contains a similar description:

> Or do you not know that the unrighteous will not inherit the kingdom of God? Do not be deceived; neither fornicators, nor idolaters, nor adulterers, nor effeminate, nor homosexuals, nor thieves, nor the covetous, nor drunkards, nor revilers, nor swindlers, will inherit the kingdom of God. Such were some of you....

I do not want God to have that opinion of me, and I am sure that you do not either. Neither do I want to forfeit my inheritance in the kingdom of God. Fortunately, there is hope for us! As we allow ourselves to be transformed by the Holy Spirit, our attitudes, character, and behavior will progress toward the following:

> But the fruit of the Spirit is love, joy, peace, patience, kindness, goodness, faithfulness, gentleness, self-control; against such things there is no law. [Galatians 5:22–23]

As the Holy Spirit accomplishes His work in us, He transforms us by putting to death our old ways and our old attitudes, and developing and maturing the fruit of the Spirit within us, so that 1 Corinthians 6:11b will describe us:

> …but you were washed, but you were sanctified, but you were justified in the name of the Lord Jesus Christ and in the Spirit of our God.

If the attributes of Galatians 5:22–23 are the fruit of a life that is being transformed by the Holy Spirit, then they are even more the characteristics of the Holy Spirit, the One who does the transforming. In other words, the fruit of the Spirit are part of the nature of the Holy Spirit. Jesus said that you can tell what a tree is like by sampling its fruit:

> "You will know them by their fruits. Grapes are not gathered from thorn bushes nor figs from thistles, are they? So every good tree bears good fruit, but the bad tree bears bad fruit. A good tree cannot produce bad fruit, nor can a bad tree produce good fruit…So then, you will know them by their fruits." [Matthew 7:16–18, 20]

Jesus used this same analogy when He talked about the Holy Spirit, saying:

> "Whoever speaks a word against the Son of Man, it shall be forgiven him; but whoever speaks against the Holy Spirit, it shall not be forgiven him, either in this age or in the age to come. Either make the tree good, and its fruit good, or make the tree bad and its fruit bad; for the tree is known by its fruit." [Matthew 12:32–33]

Jesus compared the Holy Spirit to an entirely good tree, and the fruit that the Holy Spirit bears is entirely good. It is extremely important that we understand and believe that.

When we bought our home near Orlando, Florida, there were four young citrus trees on the property. I was very excited. I can still remember my teacher in elementary school reading a story to our class that described orange trees growing in Spain. The story said that in the springtime there was ripe fruit on the trees while the trees were in flower. Since that time, I had always wanted to have my own orange trees.

When we moved into our Florida home in June of 1997, we found that three of the four trees had fruit on them. We could easily tell what type of trees we had by the fruit that they bore. The dimples at the bottoms of the fruit on one of the trees showed that the tree was a navel orange. Similarly, I could tell from the shape of the fruit on another tree, and the fact that some of them grew in clusters of two or three, that this was a grapefruit tree. When the grapefruit ripened the following January, we cut one open and discovered it was a pink seedless. This is one of the choicest varieties of grapefruit. The people from whom we bought the house said they thought the third tree was a Valencia orange, which it turned out to be. Valencia oranges ripen in late spring, and they make superb orange juice. That was probably the variety of orange tree that was described in the story that I remembered.

The fourth tree was supposed to be a Key lime tree. This was going to be a real prize, for they are rare in Central Florida, not being sufficiently cold-hardy to live here without special protection in the winter. Key lime pie is a featured dessert in many restaurants. The tree had no fruit and it was very thorny, but it seemed to be growing well, with multiple trunks coming up from near the ground. The following spring it did not bloom, but it continued to grow vigorously. I was very hopeful.

In the spring of 1999, it had a few blooms. Several months later, I noticed some green fruit on tree. Now I became really excited. Over the ensuing months, I kept careful watch over them. Their skins were a little rough. The fruit continued to increase in size and became larger than a Key lime should be. Finally, the first one began to turn yellow. Key limes turn yellow when they are ripe, so I took the first precious fruit into the house and cut it open. What a disappointment! It was not a Key lime at all; it was a sour orange and was worthless! The Key lime tree, like other citrus trees, had been grafted onto sour orange root stock. A freeze had undoubtedly killed the Key lime above the graft. The sour orange root stock had sprouted and grown. A tree is known by its fruit: a sour orange tree does not produce Key limes. I cut the tree down and dug up the stump and the extensive root system. Then I bought and planted a Key lime tree, which now provides us with fruit to use and to give away.

I have heard Bible teachers compare the fruit of the Holy Spirit to an orange. An orange is one fruit, yet it contains individual sections. When the fruit grows properly, all the sections grow at the same rate. Furthermore, the fruit is incomplete if some of its sections are either missing or are underdeveloped. Immature oranges are sour, but when an orange has developed to its full maturity and ripeness, it can be very sweet. So it is with the fruit of the Holy Spirit: it is very sweet when it is fully mature.

As we examine the fruit of the Holy Spirit, notice how desirable those qualities, or character traits, are for us Christians to exhibit to the world. Notice also how many of the fruit address the way in which we, as Christians, ought to behave toward other people.

17–2

THE FRUIT OF THE SPIRIT — LOVE

God, through the Holy Spirit, is our source of love. Our love for other people is to be an extension, or manifestation, of God's love for them, "…**The love of God** has been poured out within our hearts through the Holy Spirit who was given to us" (Romans 5:5b).

God is love. The following verses give us a picture of that aspect of God, as they describe what real love, meaning God's love, looks like:

> **Love** is patient, **love** is kind and is not jealous; **love** does not brag and is not arrogant, does not act unbecomingly; it does not seek its own, is not provoked, does not take into account a wrong suffered, does not rejoice in unrighteousness, but rejoices with the truth; bears all things, believes all things, hopes all things, endures all things. [1 Corinthians 13:4–7]

In our own strength, we cannot develop these characteristics of love, although we can and should measure our love for others against them. As the Holy Spirit develops the fruit of love within us, He transforms our human love into the kind of love that God has. As we allow God's love in us to flow to other people, it will manifest itself in those ways.

17–3

THE FRUIT OF THE SPIRIT—JOY

When it comes to joy, many people have an erroneous picture of Jesus, perhaps because of the influence of preaching and teaching about the events surrounding His crucifixion. We need to correct our image of Him because, other than those few days, He was a man of joy. Even during the time of crucifixion, the Bible says that He willingly endured the agony and shame of the cross because of the joy that was set before Him.

> …fixing our eyes upon Jesus, the author and perfecter of faith, who for the **joy** set before Him endured the cross, despising the shame, and has sat down at the right hand of the throne of God. [Hebrews 12:2]

Jesus could not have been other than a man of joy because He was continually in the presence of the Father. Psalm 16:11 says:

> You will make known to me the path of life;
> In Your presence is **fullness of joy;**
> In Your right hand there are pleasures forever.

In John 15:11, Jesus told His disciples, "These things I have spoken to you **so that My joy may be in you,** and that **your joy** may be made full." In John 17:13, Jesus prayed to the Father: "But now I come to You; and these things I speak in the world so that **they may have My joy** made full in themselves."

Heaven is a place of joy, as Jesus described it in Luke 15:7, "I tell you that in the same way, there will be more **joy** in heaven over one sinner who repents than over ninety-nine righteous persons who need no repentance." Jesus said again in Luke 15:10, "In the same way, I tell you, there is **joy** in the presence of the angels of God over one sinner who repents." Luke 24:41 refers to the disciples' overwhelming joy in seeing the risen Jesus, "While they still could not believe it because of their **joy** and amazement, He said to them, 'Have you anything here to eat?'" Luke 24:52 mentions the disciples' joy after Jesus' ascension, "And they, after worshiping Him, returned to Jerusalem with **great joy.**"

The Greek word being used here for joy is *chara*, meaning "joy, delight." It comes from the Greek word *chairo*, meaning "to rejoice, to be glad."* Isn't it wonderful to know that joy is a fruit of the Spirit! As the Holy Spirit transforms us, we become more joyful. Our joy, our exuberance, and our delight in God, in Jesus, in the Holy Spirit, and in life increase. As we become more and more filled with the Holy Spirit, we become more and more filled with joy.

17–4

THE FRUIT OF THE SPIRIT — PEACE

God is a God of peace. He is a source of our peace, "Now **the God of peace** be with you all. Amen" (Romans 15:33). Jesus is also a source of our peace, for He said: "**Peace** I leave with you; **My peace I give to you;** not as the world gives do I give to you Do not let your heart be troubled, nor let it be fearful" (John 14:27).

Jesus also said:

> "These things I have spoken to you, so that **in Me you may have peace.**
> In the world you have tribulation, but take courage; I have overcome the
> world." [John 16:33]

The peace of God, the peace that Jesus offers us, is an imperturbable tranquility. It is a serenity, a calmness, and a contentedness that is independent of the circumstances that we may face. It is the opposite of being troubled: "Do not let your heart be troubled." It is the opposite of fearfulness and dread: "nor let it be fearful." This peace facilitates courage in the face of trials and tribulations: "In the world you have tribulation, but take courage; I have overcome the world."

Our peace grows as we commune with Jesus and with the Holy Spirit and receive peace from them:

---

* Babylon, Ltd., *Chara; Chairo.*

So Jesus said to them again, "**Peace be with you;** as the Father has sent Me, I also send you." And when He had said this, He breathed on them and said to them, "Receive the Holy Spirit." [John 20:21–22]

Paul wrote that experiencing peace is also a result of rejoicing (expressing our joy) in the Lord with prayer and thankfulness:

Rejoice in the Lord always; again I will say, rejoice! Let your gentle spirit be known to all men. The Lord is near. Be anxious for nothing, but in everything by prayer and supplication with thanksgiving let your requests be made known to God. And **the peace of God**, which surpasses all comprehension, will guard your hearts and your minds in Christ Jesus. [Philippians 4:4–7]

Peace and joy characterize the lives of those who live in the kingdom of God under the leadership of the Holy Spirit, "…for the kingdom of God is not eating and drinking, but righteousness and **peace and joy in the Holy Spirit**" (Romans 14:17).

The peace and joy that we have inside of ourselves will inevitably show on our countenances.

17–5

THE FRUIT OF THE SPIRIT — PATIENCE

Patience is tolerance and forbearance. It is a quality that God continually displays toward all people, even rebellious sinners, "**The patience of God** kept waiting in the days of Noah…" (1 Peter 3:20b).

Or do you think lightly of the riches of **His** kindness and tolerance and **patience**, not knowing that the kindness of God leads you to repentance? [Romans 2:4]

What if **God**, although willing to demonstrate His wrath and to make His power known, **endured with much patience** vessels of wrath prepared for destruction? And He did so to make known the riches of His glory upon vessels of mercy…even us, whom He also called…[Romans 9:22–24a]

The Lord is not slow about His promise, as some count slowness, but **is patient toward you**, not wishing for any to perish but for all to come to repentance. [2 Peter 3:9]

God also wants to develop patience in us so that it characterizes our attitude toward others, "…with all humility and gentleness, **with patience,** showing tolerance for one another in love…" (Ephesians 4:2); "Love is **patient**…" (1 Corinthians 13:4a); "**Be patient** with everyone" (1 Thessalonians 5:14c).

Patience is also a result of our trusting that, no matter how the circumstances may appear to us, God has the entire universe well under control:

Rest in the Lord and **wait patiently for Him;**
Do not fret because of him who prospers in his way,
Because of the man who carries out wicked schemes…
I waited patiently for the Lord;
And He inclined to me, and heard my cry. [Psalm 37:7; 40:1]

The Lord's bond-servant must…be…**patient when wronged**…[2 Timothy 2:24]

For what credit is there if, when you sin and are harshly treated, you **endure it with patience**? But if when you do what is right and suffer for it you **patiently endure** it, this finds favor with God. For you have been called for this purpose, since Christ also suffered for you, leaving you an example for you to follow in His steps, who committed no sin, nor was any deceit found in His mouth; and while being reviled, He did not revile in return; while suffering, He uttered no threats; but kept entrusting Himself to Him who judges righteously…[1 Peter 2:20–23]

Patience is the fruit of the Holy Spirit that enables us to wait for God to work things out in His own time.

17–6

THE FRUIT OF THE SPIRIT—KINDNESS

Kindness has a very specific focus—our attitudes and our actions toward other people. Furthermore, our attitudes and actions of kindness—warm-heartedness, courtesy, consideration, and graciousness—are to be expressions of our inner nature. We are to show kindness whether the other person is deserving or not. We are to show kindness in the same way and for the same reason that God shows kindness to us. He shows kindness, not because we are deserving of it, but because it is His nature. Because kindness is part of His nature, He wants kindness to be part of our nature also, for He wants us to be like Him.

In the following passage, Jesus described how someone, acting out of kindness, behaves toward other people. As we read it together, it becomes immediately obvious that the behavior Jesus is describing is too lofty for us. We could never, in our own nature and in our own strength, behave like this and maintain an attitude of kindness throughout.

> "But I say to you who hear, love your enemies, do good to those who hate you, bless those who curse you, pray for those who mistreat you. Whoever hits you on the cheek, offer him the other also; and whoever takes your coat, do not withhold your shirt from him either. Give to everyone who asks of you, and whoever takes away what is yours, do not demand it back. Treat others the same way you want them to treat you. If you love those who love you, what credit is that to you? For even sinners love those who love them. If you do good to those who do good to you, what credit is that to you? For even sinners do the same. If you lend to those from whom you expect to receive, what credit is that to you? Even sinners lend to sinners in order to receive back the same amount. But love your enemies, and do good, and lend, expecting nothing in return; and your reward will be great, and you will be sons of the Most High; **for He Himself is kind** to ungrateful and evil men."
> [Luke 6:27–35]

As the fruit of the Holy Spirit grow within us, they crowd out our fleshly nature, and we become more like the Father, Jesus, and the Holy Spirit.

17–7

THE FRUIT OF THE SPIRIT—GOODNESS

When I think of the word *goodness*, the qualities that immediately spring to my mind are honesty, integrity, virtue, and morality—the character traits of a "good" person. So I was surprised to discover that these qualities are not at the center of the fruit of goodness. Instead, goodness refers to God's generosity, liberality, and even lavishness in providing good things for His people. Moses' father-in-law Jethro recognized this, "Jethro rejoiced over all **the goodness which the Lord had done** to Israel, in delivering them from the hand of the Egyptians" (Exodus 18:9).

Another Scripture passage in Exodus is also enlightening about the meaning of God's goodness:

> Then Moses said, "I pray You, show me Your glory!" And He said, "I Myself will make **all My goodness** pass before you, and will proclaim the name of the Lord before you; and I will be gracious to whom I will be gracious, and will show compassion on whom I will show compassion." [33:18–19]

In those verses God associates His goodness with His graciousness and His compassion.

Two verses in Nehemiah associate God's goodness with His generosity in providing good things for His people:

> They captured fortified cities and a fertile land.
> They took possession of houses full of every good thing,
> Hewn cisterns, vineyards, olive groves,
> Fruit trees in abundance.
> So they ate, were filled, and grew fat,
> And reveled in **Your great goodness**...
> With **Your great goodness** which You gave them,
> With the broad and rich land which You set before them...[Nehemiah 9:25; 9:35b, c]

Probably the most poignant illustration of God's goodness—His generosity and His liberality—is portrayed in Jesus' parable of the prodigal son. Here is how Jesus described the father's response to the return of his wayward son:

> "But while he was still a long way off, his father saw him and felt compassion for him, and ran and embraced him and kissed him. And the son said to him, 'Father, I have sinned against heaven and in your sight; I am no longer worthy to be called your son.' But the father said to his slaves, 'Quickly bring out the best robe and put it on him, and put a ring on his hand and sandals on his feet; and bring the fattened calf, kill it, and let us eat and celebrate;'" [Luke 15:20b-23]

Goodness is a quality that the Holy Spirit develops within us. Let us express it to others by being more than generous whenever we have the opportunity, being emissaries of God's goodness.

17–8

THE FRUIT OF THE SPIRIT — FAITHFULNESS

A person who is faithful is trustworthy, reliable, and steadfast; he is dependable, and he keeps his word. Faithfulness is a characteristic of God's nature:

> The Lord's lovingkindnesses indeed never cease,
> For His compassions never fail.
> They are new every morning;
> **Great is Your faithfulness.** [Lamentations 3:22–23]

God demonstrates His faithfulness by keeping His covenant:

> Know therefore that the Lord your God, He is God, **the faithful God,** who keeps His covenant and His lovingkindness to a thousandth generation with those who love Him and keep His commandments... [Deuteronomy 7:9]

He demonstrates His faithfulness by keeping His promises:

> By faith even Sarah herself received ability to conceive, even beyond the
> proper time of life, since she considered Him **faithful** who had prom-
> ised…[Hebrews 11:11]

He demonstrates His faithfulness whenever He speaks, for He speaks
only that which is true.

> And He who sits on the throne said, "Behold, I am making all things
> new." And He said, "Write, for these words are **faithful** and true."
> [Revelation 21:5]

We demonstrate our faithfulness by keeping our word. We demonstrate
our faithfulness by performing tasks that require us to be trustworthy and
dependable. Jesus illustrated such a task in His parable of the talents in
Matthew 25:14–30. He described a man who was about to leave on a journey.
The man called three of his slaves and entrusted portions of his money to
each of them. He gave five talents to the first, two talents to the second, and
one talent to the third, assigning responsibilities to them according to their
abilities. While he was away, the one who was entrusted with five talents
used them to trade and made a profit of five talents. Similarly, the one who
was entrusted with two talents used them to trade and made a profit of two
talents. When the master returned, those two slaves brought the master
his original talents plus the profits they had made. The master commended
both with identical words:

> "Well done, good and faithful slave. You were **faithful** with a few things,
> I will put you in charge of many things; enter into the joy of your master."
> [Matthew 25:21b]

One way to view this parable is that the master was conducting a character test. We can see that he already knew the relative abilities of his slaves
because he entrusted money to them upon that basis. Next the master
needed to find out how faithful his slaves were. After the slaves completed
the test and demonstrated their faithfulness in relatively small things, they
could be entrusted with much greater responsibilities. That pleased the
master very much.

Jesus summarized this quality of faithfulness when He said:

> "He who is **faithful** in a very little thing is **faithful** also in much; and
> he who is unrighteous in a very little thing is unrighteous also in much.

Therefore if you have not been **faithful** in the use of unrighteous wealth, who will entrust the true riches to you? And if you have not been **faithful** in the use of that which is another's, who will give you that which is your own?" [Luke 16:10–12]

Faithfulness is another quality that the Holy Spirit will develop in us as we cooperate with Him. As this fruit of the Spirit grows within us and we demonstrate our faithfulness in small things, God will entrust us with greater responsibilities.

17–9

THE FRUIT OF THE SPIRIT — GENTLENESS

Gentleness is another of those qualities, like goodness and kindness, that address how we treat other people. To be gentle is to be tender, compassionate, merciful, tranquil, calm, and nonaggressive. James described gentleness as one of the characteristics of godly wisdom: "But the wisdom from above is first pure, then peaceable, **gentle,** reasonable, full of mercy and good fruits, unwavering, without hypocrisy" (James 3:17).

Paul included gentleness as one of the qualifying characteristics of an overseer:

An overseer, then, must be above reproach, the husband of one wife, temperate, prudent, respectable, hospitable, able to teach, not addicted to wine or pugnacious, but **gentle,** peaceable, free from the love of money…The Lord's bond-servant must not be quarrelsome, but be kind to all, able to teach, patient when wronged, with **gentleness** correcting those who are in opposition, if perhaps God may grant them repentance leading to the knowledge of the truth, and they may come to their senses and escape from the snare of the devil, having been held captive by him to do his will. [1 Timothy 3:2–3; 2 Timothy 2:24–26]

Gentleness is to be a characteristic of every Christian: "Remind them to be subject to rulers, to authorities, to be obedient, to be ready for every good deed, to malign no one, to be peaceable, **gentle,** showing every consideration for all men" (Titus 3:1–2).

An important reason for behaving and responding with gentleness is to break the human cycle of offense, counter offense, offense again and retaliation. Gentleness does not offend; likewise, a gentle response does not incite the desire to retaliate. One of the key verses about gentleness says:

> A **gentle** answer turns away wrath,
> But a harsh word stirs up anger. [Proverbs 15:1]

Jesus recommended gentleness:

> "Blessed are the **gentle,** for they shall inherit the earth." [Matthew 5:5]

Jesus described Himself as gentle, "Take My yoke upon you and learn from Me, for **I am gentle** and humble in heart, and you will find rest for your souls" (Matthew 11:29).

Gentleness is not weakness. Jesus, who would soon be given all authority in heaven and on earth, exhibited gentleness during His triumphal entry into Jerusalem, fulfilling Zechariah's prophecy:

> "Say to the daughter of Zion,
> 'Behold your King is coming to you,
> **Gentle,** and mounted on a donkey,
> Even on a colt, the foal of a beast of burden.'" [Matthew 21:5]

Another reason that the Holy Spirit develops this fruit of the Spirit in us is so that we can minister with gentleness.

> Brethren, even if anyone is caught in any trespass, you who are spiritual, restore such a one in a spirit of **gentleness**; each one looking to yourself, so that you too will not be tempted. [Galatians 6:1]

Finally, read how Paul said we should conduct ourselves:

> Therefore I, the prisoner of the Lord, implore you to walk in a manner worthy of the calling with which you have been called, with all humility and **gentleness,** with patience, showing tolerance for one another in love, being diligent to preserve the unity of the Spirit in the bond of peace. [Ephesians 4:1–3]

17–10

THE FRUIT OF THE
SPIRIT — SELF-CONTROL

S elf-control is acting with restraint to control our will, our emotions, our impulses, and our responses. Peter described self-control as one of the steps in developing spiritual maturity.

> Now for this very reason also, applying all diligence, in your faith supply moral excellence, and in your moral excellence, knowledge, and in your knowledge, **self-control,** and in your **self-control,** perseverance, and in your perseverance, godliness, and in your godliness, brotherly kindness, and in your brotherly kindness, love. [2 Peter 1:5–7]

Paul described the life of self-control this way:

> For the grace of God has appeared, bringing salvation to all men, instructing us to deny ungodliness and worldly desires and to live sensibly, righteously and godly in the present age...[Titus 2:11–12]

Self-control is a trait that is readily observable by others.

> Therefore, since we have so great a cloud of witnesses surrounding us, let us also lay aside every encumbrance and the sin which so easily entangles us, and let us run with endurance the race that is set before us, fixing our eyes on Jesus, the author and perfecter of faith...[Hebrews 12:1–2a]

Practicing self-control is an important aspect of being led by the Holy Spirit. Instead of reacting to a perceived offense, we determine how the Holy Spirit would have us respond, and then respond in that way. Instead of succumbing to a temptation, we seek the Holy Spirit's help to overcome that temptation.

TRANSFORMATION

The fruit of the Spirit are the characteristics of a transformed life. As we are mentored and led and transformed by the Holy Spirit, we experience more of the righteousness, peace, joy, growth, accomplishment, and fulfillment that God has planned for us. Paul summed up our part in developing the fruit of the Spirit:

> So, as those who have been chosen of God, holy and beloved, put on a heart of compassion, kindness, humility, gentleness, and patience; bearing with one another, and forgiving each other, whoever has a complaint against anyone; just as the Lord forgave you, so also should you. Beyond all these things put on love, which is the perfect bond of unity. Let the peace of Christ rule in your hearts, to which indeed you were called in one body; and be thankful. [Colossians 3:12–15]

As we do our part, and as the Holy Spirit does His part, we are transformed more and more into the likeness of our Lord and Savior, Jesus Christ.

> But we all, with unveiled face, beholding as in a mirror the glory of the Lord, are being transformed into the same image from glory to glory, just as from the Lord, the Spirit. [2 Corinthians 3:18]

17–11
THE UNITY OF THE SPIRIT

The unity of the Spirit is the harmony and the cohesive sense of purpose that can exist within a church or a group of Christians when their focus is upon loving the Father, loving and serving Jesus, loving and following the Holy Spirit, loving and serving one another, and loving and reaching out to the lost. This chapter is an extension of the previous ones on the fruit of the Spirit, with a focus on interactions within the church and among Christians.

Jesus prayed that we Christians may be one:

> "I am no more in the world; and yet they themselves are in the world, and I come to You. Holy Father, keep them in Your name, the name which You have given Me, **that they may be one even as We are.**" [John 17:11]

As fellow Christians, we are one in Christ regardless of our gender, status, national origin, or whatever.

For just as we have many members in one body and all the members do not have the same function, so **we, who are many, are one body in Christ,** and individually members one of another. [Romans 12:4–5]

There is neither Jew nor Greek, there is neither slave nor free man, there is neither male nor female; for **you are all one in Christ Jesus.** [Galatians 3:28]

…a renewal in which **there is no distinction** between Greek and Jew, circumcised and uncircumcised, barbarian, Scythian, slave and freeman, but Christ is all, and in all. [Colossians 3:11]

SOURCES OF DIVISIONS

In disregard of Christ's prayer that we all be one, we Christians often do things that divide us from one another. One source of division is to strongly align ourselves and our doctrinal emphases with particular church leaders. Paul even had to correct this problem in the Corinthian church.

Now I exhort you, brethren, by the name of our Lord Jesus Christ, that you all agree and that there be no divisions among you, but that you be made complete in the same mind and in the same judgment. For I have been informed concerning you, my brethren, by Chloe's people, that there are quarrels among you. Now I mean this, that each one of you is saying, "I am of Paul," and "I of Apollos," and "I of Cephus," and "I of Christ." Has Christ been divided? Paul was not crucified for you, was he? Or were you baptized in the name of Paul? [1 Corinthians 1:10–13]

Paul attributed this tendency, not to our being spiritual, but to our being fleshly. He told us not to do it.

And I, brethren, could not speak to you as to spiritual men, but as to men of flesh, as to infants in Christ. I gave you milk to drink, not solid food; for you were not yet able to receive it. Indeed, even now you are not yet able, for you are still fleshly. For since there is jealousy and strife among you, are you not fleshly, and are you not walking like mere men? For when one says, "I am of Paul," and another, "I am of Apollos," are you not mere men? What then is Apollos? And what is Paul? Servants through whom you believed, even as the Lord gave opportunity to each one. I planted, Apollos watered, but God was causing the growth. So then neither the one who plants nor the one who waters is anything, but God who causes the growth. Now he who plants and he who waters are one; but each will receive his own reward according to his own labor. For we are God's fellow workers; you are God's field, God's building. [1 Corinthians 3:1–9]

Another source of divisions can arise from the personal scruples of those who are weak in faith, who judge others according to their own rules of moral conduct. The natural response of those being judged is to disregard or have contempt for those who are judging them:

Now accept the one who is weak in faith, but not for the purpose of passing judgment on his opinions. One person has faith that he may eat all things, but he who is weak eats vegetables only. The one who eats is not to regard with contempt the one who does not eat, and the one who does not eat is not to judge the one who eats, for God has accepted him. Who are you to judge the servant of another? To his own master he stands or falls; and he will stand, for the Lord is able to make him stand. One person regards one day above another, another regards every day alike. [Romans 14:1–5a]

Preventing Divisions

The solution to our tendencies to cause divisions over lifestyle issues is to permit each person to follow his or her own conscience and the leading of the Holy Spirit.

Each person must be fully convinced in his own mind. He who observes the day, observes it for the Lord, and he who eats, does so for the Lord, for he gives thanks to God; and he who eats not, for the Lord he does not eat, and gives thanks to God. For not one of us lives for himself, and not one dies for himself; for if we live, we live for the Lord, or if we die, we die for the Lord; therefore whether we live or die, we are the Lord's. For to this end Christ died and lived again, that He might be Lord both of the dead and of the living. But you, why do you judge your brother? Or you again, why do you regard your brother with contempt? For we will all stand before the judgment seat of God. For it is written,

"As I live, says the Lord, every knee shall bow to me,
and every tongue shall give praise to God."

> So then each one of us will give an account of himself to God.
> [Romans 14:5b-12]

Another way that we can prevent divisions is by being careful not to deliberately offend our Christian brothers and sisters by "asserting our rights." Likewise, we must not take offense at what other Christians may say or do to us, whether they seem to be doing it deliberately or unintentionally. Instead, we are to love and forgive, be peacemakers, and work to edify and build each other up, not criticize or tear each other down.

> Blessed are the gentle, for they shall inherit the earth.
> Blessed are the merciful, for they shall receive mercy.
> Blessed are the peacemakers, for they shall be called the sons of God.
> [Matthew 5:5; 5:7; 5:9]

> Therefore let us not judge one another anymore, but rather determine this—not to put an obstacle or a stumbling block in a brother's way. I know and am convinced in the Lord Jesus that nothing is unclean in itself; but to him who thinks anything to be unclean, to him it is unclean. For if because of food your brother is hurt, you are no longer walking according to love. Do not destroy with your food him for whom Christ died. Therefore do not let what is for you a good thing be spoken of as evil; for the kingdom of God is not eating and drinking, but righteousness and peace and joy in the Holy Spirit. For he who in this way serves Christ is acceptable to God and approved by men. So then we pursue the things which make for peace and the building up of one another. Do not tear down the work of God for the sake of food. All things indeed are clean, but they are evil for the man who eats and gives offense. It is good not to eat meat or to drink wine, or to do anything by which your brother stumbles. The faith which you have, have as your own conviction before God. Happy is he who does not condemn himself in what he approves. But he who doubts is condemned if he eats, because his eating is not from faith; and whatever is not from faith is sin.
>
> Now we who are strong ought to bear the weaknesses of those without strength and not just please ourselves. Each of us is to please his neighbor for his good, to his edification. For even Christ did not please Himself; but it is written, "The reproaches of those who reproached You fell on Me." For whatever was written in earlier times was written for our instruction, so that through perseverance and the encouragement of the Scriptures we might have hope. Now may the God who gives perseverance and encouragement grant you to be of the same mind

with one another according to Christ Jesus, so that **with one accord** you may with one voice glorify the God and Father of our Lord Jesus Christ.

Therefore, **accept one another,** just as Christ also accepted us to the glory of God. [Romans 14:13–15:7]

Unity

Because of our differences in age, gender, personality, viewpoint, level of spiritual maturity, etc., establishing and maintaining the unity of the Spirit within the church is not easy. Nevertheless, it is what the Lord desires, so we must each do our part.

Therefore I, the prisoner of the Lord, implore you to walk in a manner worthy of the calling with which you have been called, with all humility and gentleness, with patience, showing tolerance to one another in love, **being diligent to preserve the unity of the Spirit** in the bond of peace. [Ephesians 4:1–3]

Therefore if there is any encouragement in Christ, if there is any consolation of love, if there is any fellowship of the Spirit, if any affection and compassion, make my joy complete by being of the same mind, maintaining the same love, united in spirit, intent on one purpose. Do nothing from selfishness or empty conceit, but with humility of mind regard one another as more important than yourselves; **do not merely look out for your own personal interests, but also for the interests of others.** [Philippians 2:1–4]

So, as those who have been chosen of God, holy and beloved, put on a heart of compassion, kindness, humility, gentleness, and patience; bearing with one another, and forgiving each other, whoever has a complaint against anyone; just as the Lord forgave you, so also should you. Beyond all these things **put on love, which is the perfect bond of unity.** [Colossians 3:12–14]

Let all that you do be done in love. [1 Corinthians 16:14]

THE FELLOWSHIP OF THE HOLY SPIRIT

18–1

INDIVIDUAL FELLOWSHIP BETWEEN MOSES AND GOD

To me one of the most fascinating ideas in the Bible is found in the last verse of 2 Corinthians, "The grace of the Lord Jesus Christ, and the love of God, and **the fellowship of the Holy Spirit,** be with you all" (2 Corinthians 13:14).

The question that intrigued me for so long was this: what is the fellowship of the Holy Spirit? I now believe that the answer is two-fold: there is individual fellowship with the Holy Spirit and there is group fellowship with the Holy Spirit. The Bible contains two marvelous examples of individual fellowship: Moses and God in the Old Testament, and the Apostle John and Jesus in the New Testament.

Moses' introduction to God occurred during the incident at the burning bush:

> Now Moses was pasturing the flock of Jethro his father-in-law, the priest of Midian; and he led the flock to the west side of the wilderness and came to Horeb, the mountain of God. The angel of the Lord appeared to him in a blazing fire from the midst of a bush; and he looked, and behold, the bush was burning with fire, yet the bush was not consumed. So Moses said, "I must turn aside now and see this marvelous sight, why the bush is not burned up." When the Lord saw that he turned aside to look, God called to him from the midst of the bush and said, "Moses, Moses!" And he said, "Here I am." Then He said, "Do not come near here; remove your sandals from your feet, for the place on which you are standing is holy ground." He also said, "I am the God of your father, the God of Abraham, the God of Isaac, and the God of Jacob." Then Moses hid his face, for he was afraid to look at God. [Exodus 3:1–6]

That dramatic event was Moses' initial encounter with God. God commissioned Moses to travel to Egypt and demand that Pharaoh release the people of Israel. During his time in Egypt, especially during the ten plagues, Moses had frequent conversations with God, receiving instructions for what to do and say next.

After Pharaoh released Israel, Moses led the Israelites out of Egypt. God went with them in the form of a pillar of cloud during the daytime and a pillar of fire at night. They journeyed to Horeb, also called Mount Sinai, the place where Moses had first met God:

> The Lord said to Moses, "Behold, I will come to you in a thick cloud, so **that the people may hear when I speak with you…**"
>   The Lord came down on Mount Sinai, to the top of the mountain; and the Lord called Moses to the top of the mountain, and Moses went up. [Exodus 19:9a, 20]

That was when God spoke the Ten Commandments to Moses, and the people of Israel heard God as thunder and trumpet blasts. One of the most regrettable incidents in the Bible happened next. Instead of overflowing with joy and thanksgiving at hearing God speak to them and at experiencing the awesomeness of His presence, the Israelites became afraid. They withdrew and resolved that they never again wanted to hear God speak to them:

> All the people perceived the thunder and the lightning flashes and the sound of the trumpet and the mountain smoking; and when the people saw it, they trembled and stood at a distance. Then they said to Moses, "Speak to us yourself and we will listen; but let not God speak to us, or we will die."…So the people stood at a distance, while Moses approached the thick cloud where God was. [Exodus 20:18–19, 21]

God was the God of Israel, but He wanted to be more than just a God to the masses. He wanted to be a personal God to each Israelite, as He had been to Abraham, Isaac, and Jacob. However, He reluctantly acquiesced to their request. They would no longer hear His voice, nor would they be allowed to approach Him directly. But Moses would! From Exodus 20:22 through 23:33, God spoke His ordinances to Moses.

Then God reached out to Israel again but this time just to the elders, and with limitations:

> Then He said to Moses, "Come up to the Lord, you and Aaron, Nadab and Abihu **and seventy of the elders of Israel,** and you shall worship at a distance. Moses alone, however, shall come near to the Lord, but they shall not come near, nor shall the people come up with him." [Exodus 24:1–2]

Amazingly, God let everyone who came up see Him:

> Then Moses went up with Aaron, Nadab and Abihu, and seventy of the elders of Israel, and **they saw the God of Israel;** and under His feet there appeared to be a pavement of sapphire, as clear as the sky itself. Yet He did not stretch out His hand against the nobles of the sons of Israel; and **they saw God,** and they ate and drank. [Exodus 24:9–11]

For the elders, their time in God's immediate presence was a once-in-a-lifetime experience. Afterward they would see Him only at a distance. In contrast, Moses' relationship with God advanced to a new level:

> Now the Lord said to Moses, "**Come up to Me** on the mountain and remain there, and I will give you the stone tablets with the law and commandment which I have written for their instruction."
>
> Then Moses went up to the mountain, and the cloud covered the mountain. The glory of the Lord rested on Mount Sinai, and the cloud covered it for six days; and on the seventh day **He called to Moses** from the midst of the cloud. And to the eyes of the sons of Israel the appearance of the glory of the Lord was like a consuming fire on the mountain top. Moses entered the midst of the cloud as he went up the mountain; and Moses was on the mountain forty days and forty nights. [Exodus 24:12, 15–18]

That mountain-top experience forever changed Moses' relationship with God. Their relationship became both personal and intimate, and they regularly met in fellowship.

> Now Moses used to take the tent and pitch it outside the camp, a good distance from the camp, and he called it the tent of meeting.
>
> Whenever Moses entered the tent, the pillar of cloud would descend and stand at the entrance of the tent; and **the Lord would speak with Moses.**
>
> Thus the Lord used to speak to Moses face-to-face, just as a man speaks to his friend. [Exodus 33:7a, 9, 11a]

Their private fellowship was precious to both of them. God described it this way:

> He said, "Hear now My words:
> If there is a prophet among you,
> I, the Lord, shall make Myself known to him in a vision.
> I shall speak to him in a dream.

> Not so, with My servant Moses,
> He is faithful in all My household;
> **With him I speak mouth to mouth,**
> Even openly, and not in dark sayings,
> And he beholds the form of the Lord." [Numbers 12:6–8a]

Isn't that marvelous? What a relationship they had! What close fellowship! What an amazing transformation from the time of the burning bush (Exodus 3:6) when Moses was afraid to look at God. The book of Deuteronomy concludes by saying:

> Since that time no prophet has risen in Israel like **Moses, whom the Lord knew face-to-face**…[Deuteronomy 34:10]

18–2

INDIVIDUAL FELLOWSHIP BETWEEN JOHN AND JESUS

Of all Jesus' disciples, John had the most intimate relationship with Him. Jesus took Peter, James, and John with Him when He raised Jairus' daughter from the dead. He took Peter, James, and John with Him up the mount of transfiguration. In his description of the Last Supper, John commented on his relationship to Jesus, "There was reclining on Jesus' breast **one of His disciples, whom Jesus loved**" (John 13:23).

From the cross, Jesus, as the eldest son, entrusted His mother Mary, not to one of His brothers, but to John:

> When Jesus then saw His mother, and **the disciple whom He loved** standing nearby, He said to His mother, "Woman, behold, your son!" Then He said to the disciple, "Behold, your mother!" From that hour the disciple took her into his own household. [John 19:26–27]

The gospels of Matthew, Mark, and Luke have remarkable similarities, describing many of the same events and in much the same way. John's gospel, however, is strikingly different from the other three. John described things that are not included in the other gospels, events such as Jesus' conversation with Nicodemus, His conversation with the Samaritan woman at Jacob's well, and His confrontation with the scribes and Pharisees over the woman caught in adultery. It has five chapters dedicated to the things that Jesus said and did during the Last Supper.

John's gospel and his three letters reveal how profoundly he understood and accepted Jesus' love, and how deeply he loved Jesus. In John's first letter, he used the word love more than thirty-five times, including:

> Beloved, let us love one another, for love is from God; and everyone who loves is born of God and knows God.
> In this is love, not that we loved God, but that He loved us and sent His son to be the propitiation for our sins.
> We love, because He first loved us. [1 John 4:7, 10, 19]

The love between Jesus and John, and their close fellowship, did not cease with Jesus' return to heaven. That is why John could exhort us to develop that same kind of intimacy and fellowship with Jesus:

> What was from the beginning, what we have heard, what we have seen with our eyes, what we have looked at and touched with our hands, concerning the Word of Life…what we have seen and heard we proclaim to you also, so that you too may have fellowship with us; and indeed **our fellowship is with the Father, and with His Son Jesus Christ.** [1 John 1:1, 3]

John then described some of the characteristics of that fellowship:

> This is the message we have heard from Him and announce to you, that God is Light, and in Him there is no darkness at all. If we say that **we have fellowship with Him** and yet walk in the darkness, we lie and do not practice the truth; but if we walk in the Light as He Himself is in the Light, we have fellowship with one another, and the blood of Jesus His Son cleanses us from all sin. [1 John 1:5–7]

Paul also mentioned that kind of fellowship:

> God is faithful, through whom **you were called into fellowship with His Son,** Jesus Christ our Lord. [1 Corinthians 1:9]

18–3

INDIVIDUAL AND GROUP FELLOWSHIP BETWEEN US AND THE HOLY SPIRIT

We can benefit from two kinds of fellowship with the Holy Spirit: individual and group.

INDIVIDUAL FELLOWSHIP

How can we enjoy the kind of individual fellowship that Moses enjoyed with God and that John enjoyed with Jesus? Our fellowship with the Father and with Jesus is an outgrowth of our fellowship with the Holy Spirit. Our fellowship with the Holy Spirit is the natural continuation of the way we get to know Him, which I described in an earlier chapter. We fellowship with Him by getting away from distractions and interruptions, asking Him to make His presence real to us, and expressing to Him that we desire to fellowship with Him. He will honor our request. Next we read the Bible, remembering that He inspired every writer. When something we read seems to be really speaking to us, we pause and think about it. We paraphrase it back to the Holy Spirit, "Does this mean…?" Then we listen in the quietness of our hearts and minds for His responses. Finally, we follow up on whatever He says. As we spend time fellowshipping with Him in this way, we get to know Him even better.

GROUP FELLOWSHIP

Group fellowship with the Holy Spirit has the added dimension of fellowship with other believers:

> Therefore if there is any encouragement in Christ, if there is any consolation of love, if there is any **fellowship of the Spirit**, if any affection and compassion, make my joy complete by being of the same mind, maintaining the same love, united in spirit, intent on one purpose. [Philippians 2:1–2]

We can experience that fellowship during times of group prayer. Jesus taught:

"Again I say to you, that if two of you agree on earth about anything that they may ask, it shall be done for them by My father who is in heaven. For where two or three have gathered together in My name, I am there in their midst."…"I am with you always, even to the end of the age." [Matthew 18:19–20; 28:20b]

We can experience group fellowship with the Holy Spirit as we study the Bible together.

They were continually devoting themselves to the apostles' teaching and to **fellowship,** to the breaking of bread and to prayer. [Acts 2:42]

Times of corporate praise and worship also create the conditions for fellowship with the Spirit.

Shout joyfully to the Lord, all the earth.
Serve the Lord with gladness;
Come before Him with joyful singing.
Enter His gates with thanksgiving,
And His courts with praise.
Give thanks to Him, bless His name. [Psalm 100:1–2, 4]

God is spirit, and those who worship Him must worship in spirit and truth. [John 4:24]

…for we are the true circumcision, who worship in the Spirit of God, and glory in Christ Jesus and put no confidence in the flesh… [Philippians 3:3]

As we fellowship with the Holy Spirit and as we fellowship with one another in His presence, He teaches us, encourages us, helps us, motivates us, leads us, ministers to and through us, and continues transforming us into the likeness of Jesus Christ:

Beloved, now are we children of God, and it has not appeared as yet what we will be. We know that when He appears, we will be like Him, because we will see Him just as He is. [1 John 3:2]

But we all, with unveiled face, beholding as in a mirror the glory of the Lord, are being transformed into the same image from glory to glory, just as from the Lord, the Spirit. [2 Corinthians 3:18]

The grace of the Lord Jesus Christ, and the love of God, and **the fellow-ship of the Holy Spirit,** be with you all. [2 Corinthians 13:14]

HOW TO RECEIVE
THE HOLY SPIRIT

19–1

HAVE YOU RECEIVED THE HOLY SPIRIT SINCE YOU BELIEVED?

It happened that while Apollos was at Corinth, Paul passed through the upper country and came to Ephesus, and found some disciples. He said to them, "**Did you receive the Holy Spirit when you believed?**" And they said to him, "No, we have not even heard whether there is a Holy Spirit." And he said, "Into what then were you baptized?" And they said, "Into John's baptism." Paul said, "John baptized with the baptism of repentance, telling the people to believe in Him who was coming after him, that is, in Jesus." When they heard this, they were baptized in the name of the Lord Jesus. And when Paul had laid his hands upon them, the Holy Spirit came on them, and they began speaking with tongues and prophesying. [Acts 19:1–6]

In another translation, Paul asked, "Have you received the Holy Spirit since you believed?" I pose that question to you now, dear reader, "Have you? Has Jesus baptized you with the Holy Spirit?" If your answer is "No," "I don't know," or "I'm not sure," then the next question that I have for you is, "Are you thirsty?"

Now on the last day, the great day of the feast, Jesus stood and cried out, saying, "If anyone is thirsty, let him come to Me and drink. He who believes in Me, as the Scripture said, 'From His innermost being will flow rivers of living water.'" But this He spoke of the Spirit, whom those who believed in Him were to receive; for the Spirit was not yet given, because Jesus was not yet glorified. [John 7:37–39]

Do you desire to receive the baptism with the Holy Spirit so that you may grow spiritually, be led by the Holy Spirit, and minister in His power? If your answer is yes, then your next step is to ask the Father in prayer, for Jesus said:

"If you then, being evil, know how to give good gifts to your children, how much more will your heavenly Father give the Holy Spirit to those who ask Him?" [Luke 11:13]

Jesus generally baptizes people with the Holy Spirit, in response to prayer, in one of the following situations:

- You are by yourself and you pray.
- You are with one or more Christians who have been baptized with the Holy Spirit, and they lay hands upon you and pray.
- You are in a church service and the pastor or evangelist leads a group prayer.

Select whichever setting makes you the most comfortable. Then ask in prayer and receive the Holy Spirit, a magnificent gift to you from your loving heavenly Father, bestowed through the hands of the Lord Jesus Christ!

Your baptism with the Holy Spirit will open your eyes and your heart to new insights from the Bible into the nature of the Father, Jesus, and the Holy Spirit. It will revitalize your spiritual growth and your transformation into the likeness of Jesus. Finally, it will make new spiritual resources available to you so that you can minister more effectively to the needs of others through the leading and the power of the Holy Spirit.

SCRIPTURE INDEX

OLD TESTAMENT

ABOUT THE AUTHOR

Eugene H. Lowe has three degrees in electrical engineering: a doctorate from the Georgia Institute of Technology (1970), a master's from the University of Southern California (1967), and a bachelor's degree from Louisiana Tech University (1965). Dr. Lowe has nearly forty years of experience in the high-tech world of systems engineering. His thorough and analytical approach to his work and life influences his writing and research. He has worked on projects for the United States Air Force, Army, and Navy while employed by corporations that support the United States government.

Gene was raised in the liturgical tradition of the Episcopal Church. In college he met Brenda, a Southern Baptist girl, now his wife of forty-three years, with whom he has one son. Gene committed his life to the Lord in 1967, and both he and his wife were baptized with the Holy Spirit in 1971. That inaugurated a dynamic period of Bible study and personal growth that has continued to the present. Gene and Brenda have been members at various times of the Methodist Church, the Assemblies of God, and the Church of God.

Gene's relationship with the Lord is intimate and personal. He has a passion for knowing and fellowshipping with the Lord, for reading and understanding the Bible, and for worship through music whether alone, in small groups, or in church. This book is an outgrowth of his years of reading the Bible together with his continual fellowship with the Lord.

Gene has a gift for recognizing the most significant ideas in important subjects, and then presenting those ideas in a clear, inspirational, and easily understandable manner. He says, "My objective is much more than merely presenting biblical truth. My heart's desire is to present biblical truth in such a way that it touches the reader's heart and draws him toward a closer relationship with the Father, Jesus, and the Holy Spirit."

BIBLIOGRAPHY

Babylon Translation Software. (Babylon Ltd., 1997-2009), http://www.babylon.com/.

Merriam Webster Online Dictionary. (Merriam Webster, Inc., 2009), http://www.merriam-webster.com/.

New American Standard Bible. La Habra, CA: The Lockman Foundation, 1995.

Wikipedia: The Free Encyclopedia. (Wikimedia Foundation, Inc., 2009), http://en.wikipedia.org/wiki/English_versions_of_the_Nicene_Creed_in_current_use.

EUGENE LOWE WEB SITE

To purchase additional copies of The Holy Spirit at Work in You, go to www.TheHolySpiritatWorkinYou.com or www.amazon.com.

If you would like to have Dr. Lowe speak at your church, conduct a seminar, do a media interview, or sign books, you may contact him at **(407) 739-0516** or **Genelowe@theholyspiritatworkinyou.com**.